TRANSFORMATIONAL LEADERSHIP

DR. GEORGE AGBONSON

Transformational Leadership
Dr. George Agbonson
Copyright © 2012 by Christ Restoration Publications

All rights reserved. No part of this book may be reproduced or transmitted in any form or by any means without written permission from the author.

Christ Restoration Publications
4756 N. 70th Ave. Phoenix, AZ 85033
www.christrestoration.net

Printed in the United States of America

Unless otherwise noted, all Scripture is taken from the New King James Version copyright © 1982 Thomas Nelson, Inc. Used by permission. All rights reserved.
Scriptures marked TNIV are taken from HOLY BIBLE, TODAY'S NEW INTERNATIONAL VERSION® TNIV® Copyright © 2001, 2005 by Biblica®. All rights reserved worldwide.
Scriptures marked GOD'S WORD are taken from GOD'S WORD®, © 1995 God's Word to the Nations. Used by permission of Baker Publishing Group.
Scriptures marked KJV are from the King James Version. Public Domain

*Scripture text in bold is the emphasis of the author.

TABLE OF CONTENT

FOREWARD..ix
INTRODUCTION..x
PART ONE: THE CALL TO LEAD......................11
Chapter One: Leadership Defined................................12
Chapter Two: Leadership Is A Privilege......................17
Chapter Three: Leadership Is Servant Hood................24
Chapter Four: Leadership Is Influence........................32

PART TWO: ACCORDING TO DIVINE PATTERN
Chapter One: Understanding Your Calling..................40
Chapter Two: Leadership Training..............................51
Chapter Three: Tradition or Relevance?......................69

PART THREE: PEOPLES' MANAGEMENT
Chapter One: Divine Helpers
Chapter Two: Leadership Empowerment
Chapter Three: Delegation, the Art of Leadership

PART FOUR: ORGANIZATIONAL MANAGEMENT
Chapter One: Orderliness is Important
Chapter Two: Divine Hierarchy
Chapter Three: Building Relationships
Chapter Four: Preserving The Vision

FOREWARD

Transformational Leaders, by definition, seek to transform. The Wikipedia encyclopedia states that transformational leadership enhances the motivation, morale and performance of followers through a variety of mechanisms. These include connecting the follower's sense of identity and self to the mission and the collective identity of the organization; being a role model for followers that inspires them; challenging followers to take greater ownership for their work, and understanding the strengths and weaknesses of followers, so the leader can align followers with tasks that optimize their performance. Transformational leadership is a type of leadership style that leads to positive changes in those who follow. Transformational leaders are generally energetic, enthusiastic and passionate. Not only are these leaders concerned and involved in the process; they are also focused on helping every member of the group succeed as well.

In conclusion, this form of leadership takes place when the leader takes a visionary position and inspires people to follow. Thus, the goal of transformational leaders is to inspire followers to share the leader's values and connect with the leader's vision. This connection is manifested through the genuine concern the leaders have for their followers and the followers giving their trust in return.

In this hour, there is a great need for transformational leaders. There has arisen one who walks in Kingdom authority and power. Called to be an Apostle of God, George Agbonson writes with great passion and anointing under an apostolic mandate to bring reformation and transformation to the Body of Christ.

It is with honor and a great sense of responsibility that I commend this book written by my son in the Gospel. As you read the pages of this book, you will find that it is not merely a book but a training manual and empowerment resource to the Body of Christ all over the earth.

I decree that this book will fulfill the assignment for which our Sovereign God has sent it forth and that Apostle George Agbonson, his family, ministry and the lives of all those who diligently study and apply the principles in this book will be touched and transformed forever, Amen.

Apostle Dr. Veronica A. Johnson
Founder and Overseer
Rapha Outreach International
World Missions Ministerial Association
New Covenant International Bible College
Decatur, AL USA

INTRODUCTION

Everything rises and falls on leadership. The success, failures of anyone, company, organization, society, rests primarily on the leadership. There is no better time to concentrate on the subject of transformational leadership other than today. Everyone is seeking answers, people want to know which way to go, and they need direction to their destination. They seek leaders.

In today's chaotic world, where the future seems to be doomed in the eyes of many, too many failed leadership have brought doubt to the heart of followers. Leaders of nations, economy, and organizations have failed many. Many run to the church for answers, but they get disappointed, because many Pastors cannot run their churches, let alone provide answers for societal challenges.

The truth is that Leadership today is more challenging than it was a decade ago, or even a century ago. The world is changing by the day, people, societies are getting more advanced than one can fathom and it's becoming difficult to catch up with the trend of social change. It is sad that some who find themselves in leadership positions were not adequately equipped for 21st century leadership demands and roles. Some Bible Colleges and Seminaries are still archaic in Leadership Studies; they are stuck with ancient philosophies and theories that are not applicable to today's societal issues. Well we wouldn't expect more from leaders who have been trained with theories without praxis. Filled with head knowledge rather than revelation knowledge of who God is and His ways of operation.

The objective of this book is to explore leadership principles that transcends all ages and fits into any society, culture in its application. Principles that have been tested and proven all through the ages of mankind and is still very relevant today. There is no better place to seek answers, and solutions than to turn to God in his Word.

First, I must state the premise which the teachings of this book will be built upon, that is God is the Creator of the universe, and sustains the universe which He created:

> God, who at various times and in various ways spoke in time past to the fathers by the prophets, has in these last days spoken to us by His Son, whom He has appointed heir of all things, through whom also He made the worlds; who being the brightness of His glory and the express image of His person, and upholding all things by the word of His power, when He had by Himself purged our sins, sat down at the right hand of the Majesty on high.
> Hebrews 1:1-3 NKJV.

Not only is God the sustainer of the world, He is the Omniscience (all knowing), Omnipotent (all-powerful), Omnipresence (ever present) God, according to his nature. Therefore He orchestrates things according to his plans and purpose for mankind.

In every generation, when God decides to move humanity into the next phase of his plan and purpose, He raises people into leadership. Chaos, Society challenge is God's design to bring people into the places of responsibility. This generation is experiencing an unusual rise of spiritual leaders because of the heavy thick darkness that is covering the earth. The thicker the darkness the greater the light.

> Arise, shine; For your light has come!
> And the glory of the LORD is risen upon you.
> For behold, the darkness shall cover the earth,
> And deep darkness the people;
> But the LORD will arise over you
> And His glory will be seen upon you.
> Isaiah 60:1-2 NKJV.

You will agree with me that evil is increasing in an alarming rate beyond human reasoning. I believe God is calling Christians, His Church to arise to take this challenge. For this to happen, Godly leaders must be raised who understands the times and the seasons.

Research shows that more people are coming into ministry than ever before. And if they are not well prepared for the challenges that lie ahead, it will be a travesty to see that the Body of Christ whom God have given the mandate to transform mankind failed in her duties. I believe strongly as we proceed in the plans of God for mankind, **the greatest need in the Body of Christ will not be that of Power or Signs and Wonders, but of genuine leadership.**

This book will equip those God is calling to take up Kingdom assignments either within the local church or outside, leaders already in positions of responsibility, and those who wants to learn spiritual dynamics of leadership. Let's begin this journey of transformational leadership together.

PART ONE

THE CALL TO LEAD

"You did not choose Me, but I chose you and appointed you that you should go and bear fruit, and that your fruit should remain, that whatever You ask the Father in My name He may give You."
John 15:16 NKJV

CHAPTER ONE

LEADERSHIP DEFINED

God is the originator of leadership, we cannot stress that enough. He chooses those He wants to carry out divine assignments. All through Scriptures we see God doing great things, but everything God does on earth is done through those He chose. In my other book, "Destined for Greatness" I taught about how Divine Assignment places you in a leadership position which is a place of responsibility.

First, let's define "Leadership". There have been too many definitions, concepts, theories on leadership. Generally, what is common amongst many definitions is the role of the leader rather than whom and where leadership emanates. You cannot ascertain what leadership is without first understanding what a leader is. In so doing, leadership has been relegated into role playing rather than fruit bearing. That is one reason why there is so much abuse of power. People assumed positions without delivering to the people any reasonable service. Corruption is seen in the highest order amongst leaders without any remorse.

If we will truly understand what leadership is, and what it entails. We will be better off to see it from a spiritual perspective rather than a natural, philosophical view. The spirit controls the natural. If a man or woman will lead in the natural, they better be leaders in the spirit of leadership. They have to understand the power of leadership beyond the natural mind.

Spiritual leadership is who a person is. What they are called to do. What the motive is and what their goals in their leadership are. According to Henry Blackaby, *"Spiritual leadership is moving people unto God's agenda."*

Blackaby continues in his assertion, *"Spiritual leadership involves more than merely achieving goals. People can accomplish all of their goals and still not be successful in God's kingdom."* This is so true. People can be successful in the eyes of others, doesn't mean God recognizes them. This is the major difference between a natural leader and a spiritual leader.

I believe with all certainty that Spiritual Leaders are those called by God to carry out His agenda here on earth. Therefore spiritual leadership is fulfilling divine mandate on earth.

So, when someone calls themselves a leader, we will need to determine what kind of leadership they engaged in. Is he a leader from God pursuing God's agenda or is he a natural leader pursuing his own course. Or is a Satanic leader pursuing the course of the Devil.

We definitely have three kinds of leaders:

1.   Spiritual Leaders fulfilling God's agenda
2.   Spiritual Leaders fulfilling Satan's agenda
3.   Natural Leaders pursuing human agenda

It is important we know what kind of a leader a person is, when they lead. What is their purpose? What is their agenda? Understanding this will fundamentally help us to ascertain what kind of leadership expected from them. The problem with our Christianity today is that we have mingle ourselves so much with the system of the world that, we tend to apply worldly philosophies and theories that have been accepted over time as the norm for the basis of leadership. From all indications, and happenings around the world, it is no news that worldly, ungodly leadership has led us nowhere. The world is seeking for answers because the leaders have failed them. Economy of nations is not getting better. Politics has become a mind game. Education is all in theories that profit nothing other than increased theoretical knowledge with little application. Where are we going with all of these? Where are the true leaders? Will Godly leaders arise in such a time like this?

There is so much darkness in today's world just as the Bible predicted. But, in the midst of the darkness, the Light of God must shine. This is where Spiritual Leadership comes in to lead people towards God's agenda.

> Now it shall come to pass in the latter days That the mountain of the LORD's house Shall be established on the top of the mountains, And shall be exalted above the hills; And all nations shall flow to it. Many people shall come and say, Come, and let us go up to the mountain of the LORD, to the house of the God of Jacob; He will teach us His ways, And we shall walk in His paths." For out of Zion shall go forth the law, And the word of the LORD from Jerusalem. Isaiah 2:2-3 NKJV.

Unfortunately today, even those in the religious circle judge their assignment, requirements using secular, humanistic yardstick. This book will centralized more on restoring spiritual leadership back to what it should be as oppose to what it can be. The calling of the Lord is a calling to affect humanity, not to compromise the spiritual for the natural. We are to be the light in the midst of this thick darkness of today, *"Arise, shine For your light has come! And the glory of the LORD is risen upon you for behold, the darkness shall cover the earth, And deep darkness the people; But the LORD will arise over you, And His glory will be seen upon you"* Isaiah 60:1-2 NKJV.

In the next chapter we will examine some of the biblical characters in positions of leadership. And learn from their lives why & how God chooses leaders and what He expects from them. This exposition will serve as the foundational studies for the rest of this book.

CHAPTER TWO

LEADERSHIP IS A PRIVILEGE NOT A RIGHT

ADAM: Adam was the first leader recorded in the history of mankind. After creation, God wanted someone who could take responsibility over his creation. He found a leader in Adam. The highlighted verses below shows that God actually placed Adam in the position of leadership. He was to take care of the Garden:

> This is the history of the heavens and the earth when they were created, in the day that the LORD God made the earth and the heavens, before any plant of the field was in the earth and before any herb of the field had grown. For the LORD God had not caused it to rain on the earth, and there was no man to till the ground; but a mist went up from the earth and watered the whole face of the ground.
>
> And the LORD God formed man of the dust of the ground, and breathed into his nostrils the breath of life; and man became a living being. The LORD God planted a garden eastward in Eden, and there He put the man whom He had formed. And out of the ground the LORD God made every tree grow

that is pleasant to the sight and good for food. The tree of life was also in the midst of the garden, and the tree of the knowledge of good and evil. Now a river went out of Eden to water the garden, and from there it parted and became four riverheads. The name of the first is Pishon; it is the one which skirts the whole land of Havilah, where there is gold. And the gold of that land is good. Bdellium and the onyx stone are there. The name of the second river is Gihon; it is the one which goes around the whole land of Cush. The name of the third river is Hiddekel; it is the one which goes toward the east of Assyria. The fourth river is the Euphrates. **Then the LORD God took the man and put him in the garden of Eden to tend and keep it.**
Genesis 2:4-15 NKJV

Wow! What a privilege for God to count on you when He commits responsibility into your hands. Does it mean that God could not uphold what He created without the help of any man? Not really, one of God's nature is "Omniscience-All Powerful". This means, God doesn't actually need anyone's help. God actually wanted man to feel a sense of belonging, a sense of worth, partnership, ownership as a child of the Creator, just as a Prince will feel being who he is. This is clearly seen in Genesis 1:26 *"Then God said, "Let Us make man in Our **image**, according to Our **likeness**; let them have **dominion** over the fish of the sea, over the birds of the air, and over the cattle, over all the earth and over every creeping thing that creeps on the earth."*

The three highlighted words in the above verse are very significant in the makeup of man.

Image: This speaks of the nature of God in man.

Likeness: This speaks of the position God has given to man. He wants man to reign on earth as He reigns in Heaven.

Dominion: To subdue, to reign, and to exercise authority over what God has created and placed man over. So wherever God positions you is where you reign.

All of these sound like a good intention of God towards man. God is the ultimate leader, and He wants to reproduce Himself in man. That was why He gave man so much of qualities that He possesses.

It is a privilege to be called by God in a position of responsibility. Many people who assume position of leadership fail to understand this foundation and concept.

There is bound to be abuse when one does not realize the value of what have been given.

A typical example of one who took his leadership as a right rather than a privilege was King Saul.

> Now the word of the LORD came to Samuel, saying, "I greatly regret that I have set up Saul as king, for he has turned back from following Me, and has not performed My commandments." And it grieved Samuel, and he cried out to the LORD all night. So when Samuel rose early in the morning to meet Saul, it was told Samuel, saying, "Saul went to Carmel, and indeed, he set up a monument for himself; and he has gone on around, passed by, and gone down to Gilgal." Then Samuel went to Saul, and Saul said to him, "Blessed are you of the LORD! I have performed the commandment of the LORD." But Samuel said, "What then is this bleating of the sheep in my ears, and the lowing of the oxen which I hear?" And Saul said, "They have brought them from the Amalekites; for the people spared the best of the sheep and the oxen, to sacrifice to the LORD your God; and the rest we have utterly destroyed." Then Samuel said to Saul,

"Be quiet! And I will tell you what the LORD said to me last night."

And he said to him, "Speak on." So Samuel said, "When you were little in your own eyes, were you not head of the tribes of Israel? And did not the LORD anoint you king over Israel? Now the LORD sent you on a mission, and said, 'Go, and utterly destroy the sinners, the Amalekites, and fight against them until they are consumed.' Why then did you not obey the voice of the LORD? Why did you swoop down on the spoil, and do evil in the sight of the LORD?" 1 Samuel 15:10-19 NKJV.

King Saul was a typical example of those whom God chose for a specific task. God took them from a humble beginning. They were nothing, had no influence, nothing to brag about. Suddenly, they assume power and nothing counts anymore. Not even God. There is a saying, that the best way to know a genuine nature of a man is by giving him power, and money. Then the true nature will surface. It pricks the heart of God like we saw in the above verse for leaders to see their position as a right to do whatever they feel it is right, rather than see their elevation as a privilege to serve.

I once spoke to a lady who told me how she used her mom's vehicle to help a Pastor get around the city. This pastor happened to be one whom she respected so much. She would take this man to wherever he desires. One morning, around 4 am while she was still in bed. Her phone rang, it was the Pastor. He called her because he wanted her to drive him up somewhere that wasn't that important. The Pastor commanded her to do what she was told and don't ask questions. What a nerve! This man was using her for his selfish interest, because of his position. The lady eventually lost respect for this Pastor.

We see a lot of this in the Body of Christ today, people in authority using their position and influence in manipulating their followers. Somebody asked this question: Are the people that naïve? Why will they allow anyone to just use them? You wouldn't understand until you've been there. We will discuss this further in the next chapter.

A privilege is what was given without your qualification. It is a benefit, an advantage bestowed on you. That was why God emphasized in the above Scripture: "When You were little in Your own eyes". Saul wasn't qualified for the position. It was a privilege. So are many in places of authority today.

The quickest way to lose your leadership is to allow pride. *"Pride goes before destruction, And a haughty spirit before a fall."* Proverbs 16:18NKJV.

Are you a leader in any ramification? Would take time to reflect and thank God from where He took you from and where you are today?

CHAPTER THREE

LEADERSHIP IS SERVANTHOOD

The concept of servant leadership is a misconstrued subject especially in our generation. The question is how can one be a leader and a servant at the same time? This can be a very tough concept especially for those who have witnessed servitude firsthand. People like me who came from a culture where a servant hood is almost compared to slavery, one who have been stripped of all rights. A slave has no right, or choice of his own. He only does what he is told.

Biblical teaching on servant hood is quite different. And every godly, spiritual leader ought to be a servant leader. Dr. Gene Wilkes broke it down in his book, "Jesus on Leadership".

> He asserts that servant leadership begins when a leader knows, and is passionate towards his mission. He serves the mission and the people follow. "Mission is everything for the servant leader. The mission that God or someone in authority entrusts to the leader is the focus of every decision and action. True servant leadership begins when the leader humbles himself to carry out the

mission entrusted to him rather than his personal agenda."₂

Dr. Gene reveals that the mission entrusted to someone makes the person a leader. When the leader embraces the mission, it brings service. They become humble to serve the mission and all who is connected to the mission. This is how a servant leader is born. To them, the mission is everything. So when we mention the term, 'Servant Leader', **it simply means a leader who render service to people in fulfilling his mission.** In retrospect, Leadership and Service are intertwined. This means that, when someone calls himself a leader, we should look for the service they render, the mission they serve, and the people they carry along.

We see this model in the life and ministry of Jesus:

> **Jesus, knowing that the Father had given all things into His hands,** and that He had come from God and was going to God, rose from supper and laid aside His garments, took a towel and girded Himself. After that, He poured water into a basin and began to wash the disciples' feet, and to wipe them with the towel with which He was girded. Then He came to Simon Peter. And Peter said to

Him, "Lord, are You washing my feet?" Jesus answered and said to him, "What I am doing you do not understand now, but you will know after this." Peter said to Him, "You shall never wash my feet!" Jesus answered him, "If I do not wash you, you have no part with Me." Simon Peter said to Him, "Lord, not my feet only, but also my hands and my head!" Jesus said to him, "He who is bathed needs only to wash his feet, but is completely clean; and you are clean, but not all of you." For He knew who would betray Him; therefore He said, "You are not all clean." So when He had washed their feet, taken His garments, and sat down again, He said to them, "Do you know what I have done to you? You call Me Teacher and Lord, and you say well, for so I am. If I then, your Lord and Teacher, have washed your feet, you also ought to wash one another's feet. For I have given you an example, that you should do as I have done to you. Most assuredly, I say to you, a servant is not greater than his master; nor is he who is sent greater than he who sent him. If you know these things, blessed are you if you do them. John 13:3-17 NKJV.

Jesus on His way back to Heaven taught the principle of servant leadership to the disciples who would afterwards become the apostles of the church. They will assume a prominent role in the Body of Christ. Therefore, they needed to know that the calling is not about position or title but about service. He made it emphatically clear to Peter who thought it was an abomination for his master to serve him. He was told he wouldn't be part of Jesus if he is not served. Jesus not only served his mission, He served those with him in the mission.

We have too many title hungry Christians today. Too many run with all kinds of title without function. I am not against title, I bear one myself. But I believe every title should point to what you do. One should not bear the title of an office without the portfolio. Another issue is that some bear the title, claim the office they've not been anointed for, or allotted and assigned to. This can be very dangerous. We will discuss this in details subsequently.

The first highlighted verse above reads: *"Jesus, knowing that the Father had given all things into His hands, and that He had come from God and was going to God, rose from supper and laid aside His garments, took a towel and girded Himself"* vs.3-4, reveals some major ingredients for ministry and leadership:

1. Jesus knew He had all authority, meaning He knew his status and position.
2. Jesus knew where the authority came from, he was aware of the source, God.
3. Jesus knew His mission, and will go back to the one who sent Him, for accountability.
4. Jesus laid aside his garment. He laid down the pride of whom He was, and the authority He possessed. This is humility.
5. Jesus took upon Himself servant hood. This is true leadership, rendering service.

You need to understand the cultural effect of what Jesus exemplified in this story. Then you will come to the realization, the weight behind this leadership studies taught by Jesus. Craig Keener, reveals the cultural view on this:

> After travelers had come a long distance, the host was to provide water for their feet as a sign of hospitality, as exemplified by Abraham (Gen 18:4). Yet loosing sandals and personally washing

someone else's feet was considered servile, most often the work of a servant or that of very submissive wives or children.

Jesus' removing his outer garments to serve them would also appear as a sign of great humility before them. Judaism stressed humility; but like other societies, it also upheld societal roles. Jesus overturns even positions of social status. Jesus' act violates cultural status boundaries so thoroughly that Peter finds it unthinkable.[3]

Now, you see the reason why Peter was so shocked and almost refused Jesus' service. Jesus wasn't trying to be a slave. That was why the verse emphasized that, He knew that God gave him all authority, and He knew who He was. Jesus was trying to change the disciples' mindset of what they had considered servant hood. You can now connect the dot with Jesus' teaching in the gospel Mark:

But Jesus called them to Himself and said to them, You know that those who are considered rulers over the Gentiles lord it over them, and their great ones exercise authority over them. Yet it shall not be so among you; but whoever desires to become great among you shall be your servant. And whoever of you desires to be first shall be slave of all.

For even the Son of Man did not come to be served, but to serve, and to give His life a ransom for many. Mark 10:42-44 NKJV.

As I read these words of Jesus and meditate on them, I tell you, I am continually asking God to help me be the servant leader He desires me to be. I don't want to run with titles behind my name; yet I am not bearing fruit, nobody is being blessed, disciple, delivered, rose up, set free, healed, counseled. I am not serving if no one is following. What about you?

I will conclude this chapter by emphasizing the key qualities of a genuine leader deduced from the life and teaching of Jesus:

1. True leaders know they are called by God not man.
2. True leaders know they are called to serve the mission and the people.
3. True leaders know they have the authority to lead others.
4. True leaders know their authority and identity is from God.
5. True leaders know they will someday be accountable for what they do with their leadership.

6. True leaders know that humility is not stupidity. The key to greatness is humility.
7. True leaders know that God always rewards obedience, faithfulness, steadfastness, and servant hood.

CHAPTER FOUR

LEADERSHIP IS INFLUENCE

We cannot talk about leadership without talking about influence. Leadership is the ability to influence others to follow. When nobody is following, it means we are not leading. In the famous book on leadership, "Spiritual Leadership" by Oswald Sanders, Sanders gave an important quote of a great leader in China asserting that: *"There are only three kinds of people, those who are immovable, those who are movable, and those who move them. Leaders move others"*[4]

In other for a leader to move people towards any agenda, especially a godly, the leader must have the charisma, the right personality, and above all, must know how to depend on the power of the Holy Spirit to lead. This is what makes a spiritual leader unique in his role. Because we have people with all kinds of personalities, issues, low self-esteem, high self-esteem, and the in-betweens.

Dr. Sanders emphasizes on reliance on the power of the Holy Spirit as one major criteria for spiritual leadership:

> Spiritual leadership transcends the power of personality and all other natural gifts. The personality of a spiritual leader influences others because it is penetrated, saturated, and empowered by the Holy Spirit. As the leader gives control of his life to the Spirit, the Spirit's power flows through him to others.[5]

I agree totally agree with Dr. Sanders assertion, that the Holy Spirit has a major role in spiritual leadership. Because if we depend solely on our personality trait, it will mean that we are relying on our own strength. There is little the strength of man can do. There are those who believe that they are born leaders, and see their strength in their personality. Personalities are makeup of human qualities. Our temperament makes us unique.

We have two major groups of temperaments which are further divided into four. Everyone falls into one or two of these categories, which we will briefly discuss in this chapter on how it affects leadership.

The first is the Extrovert Personality. These people are outgoing, social, naturally leaders in almost every area of their lives. The Extrovert personality is further divided into 2 categories: Sanguine and Choleric.

Sanguine: Their strength and weakness is in their mouth. They are good sales people. They can market anything. They have the power to convince people to go with them, in whatever direction. When a sanguine talk, it feels so good, you want to try whatever they bring to you. They are people persons, people friendly, bubbling personality, social, never a dull moment with them, you can't beat them in an argument, and they know how to deliver speeches. God can use this people greatly, because they can be good evangelist, preacher.

These all sound very good. Because they can easily convince people, does not mean a sanguine can be a good leader. One weakness of theirs is the lack of faith to take risk. They talk more than they think. They can quit on you when you have totally relied on them. They can talk you into things, and leave you to deal with the difficult part of it. This doesn't sound like a good spiritual leader, but we have a lot of them in leadership today, from the government office to the church. People get carried away with their swaying speech; a good politician must know how to sell themselves into office. The fact that someone is rhetoric in their speech should not be the only qualifying factor for leadership.

Choleric: This is the second group in the extrovert category. These people are seen as born leaders, they easily get into leadership without having to fight their way through sometimes. The reason is because they are risk takers, they assume responsibility when nobody wants to, and they are project driven, mostly visionary. These are all good qualities for leadership. We need people who can take responsibility, vision oriented, etc. Because of their ability to take risk, they can be greatly used by God in exercising faith for great accomplishments.

But, the weakness with this category of people is that they can be people users, they can use people to attain their goals. They can be more concern with their personal achievements than other people's destinies. Their project driven energies does not make some a good managers, because they like to try new things, even at the expense of the old. Their risk taking personality makes them build self-confidence; they can rely heavily on themselves, which can disconnect them from God in their leadership eventually.

Again we have a lot of people in this category in positions of leadership in every aspect.

The second group of personality is called the Introvert group. This is the opposite of the Extrovert. They are mostly reserved, not the outgoing, bubbling, jumping personality, yet they have their strengths and weaknesses as well. They are further divided into two categories:

Melancholy: I often call this people, analyzers. They can deduce, analyze anything, anyone in a twinkling of an eye. They are not easily moved, they can be systematic in their approach to things, they are well organized, hate to do things shabbily. They are the perfectionist, they don't get satisfied easily. They like the status quo, by the book, nothing more, nothing less. This sound good for a leader, because this people can be good managers, you can trust them to deliver. God can use this people greatly to bring and maintain order.

But their greatest weakness is change. They can get stuck with the old and be unwilling to try new things. They get stuck in their ways of doing things and rely totally in their ways without the opening for the Holy Spirit. They are not flexible, they can eventually become too rigid for the Holy Spirit to use them or move them.

Phlegmatic: This fourth category is the most enclosed people you can ever meet. They are the moody, quiet, very sensitive, reserve and critical people. They are slow in making decisions. They take their time with everything. The good thing about people like this in leadership is that they can be used mightily by the Holy Spirit because of their quietness; it's easy for them to listen to the voice of the Holy Spirit than the Sanguine who is always talking. This people can flow in spiritual gifts that penetrate the deepest part of the human emotion, because they themselves can go deep in spiritual things.

But their weakness can sabotage a lot when in leadership. Their critical spirit can condemn anything. Because of their moodiness, they can hold unforgiveness in their heart for a long time. And in leadership people are bound to hurt you, offend you. They hardly let go of things that hurts them, it is hard to pull out issues bothering them from within, it takes time for them to let it out, and it requires a lot of patience. They can be slow in making decision which has its own effect too, especially when quick decision needs to be made, they can go blank in their minds.

The purpose of identifying these temperaments is to reveal that leadership should not be based on personality types alone. This is what differentiates spiritual leaders from the natural leaders. Natural Leaders depend on themselves, but Spiritual Leaders depends on the power of the Holy Spirit flowing through them, their temperaments, personality, taking hold of their strengths, and weaknesses and using it to glorify God. For further study on understanding your temperament, I wrote more on these in my previous book, "Destined for Greatness".

God wants to teach His leaders how to get out of themselves and rely totally on Him. We must lead people towards fulfilling God's purpose on earth. The only way to do that successfully is to do it in the power of the Holy Spirit.

PART TWO

ACCORDING TO DIVINE PATTERN

"And let them make Me a sanctuary, that I may dwell among them. According to all that I show you, that is, the pattern of the tabernacle and the pattern of all its furnishings, just so you shall make it."
Exodus 25:8-9 NKJV.

CHAPTER ONE

UNDERSTANDING YOUR CALL

Every call of God and every assignment from God are to address the present need of the people. Outside that is no calling at all. This buttresses what Martin Luther asserts, that "the gospel that does not address the need of the people is no gospel at all." One of the catastrophes we are experiencing in Christian leadership today is as a result of lack of understanding of what the purpose of the call to serve is. We are noticing the rise of counterfeit ministries, leaders, preachers on the scene by the day. Now, I am not talking about wolves in sheep clothing, agents of Satan, etc. I am talking about those genuinely called by God, but have missed their purpose, those who try to imitate others, their style of preaching, style of ministry. The younger Generation of Christian leaders are so vulnerable to fall into this deadly trap of the Devil, to think that the only way to be accepted is to be someone you're not. Some have gone to the extent of using the world's system of pulling others down, in other for them to climb the ladder of success. These are all strategies of the Devil to get many out of God's will for their lives.

The Call: God calls people to himself first. You have to know God for yourself before you take any assignment for Him. You cannot lead people to the God that you don't know, let alone lead people to accomplish God's project that you don't understand.

God first introduced Himself to Moses, before He gave him the commission. Take a look at this:

> Now Moses was tending the flock of Jethro his father-in-law, the priest of Midian, and he led the flock to the far side of the wilderness and came to Horeb, the mountain of God. There the angel of the LORD appeared to him in flames of fire from within a bush. Moses saw that though the bush was on fire it did not burn up. So Moses thought, "I will go over and see this strange sight—why the bush does not burn up." When the LORD saw that he had gone over to look, God called to him from within the bush, "Moses! Moses!" And Moses said, "Here I am." "Do not come any closer," God said. "Take off your sandals, for the place where you are standing is holy ground." Then he said,

"I am the God of your father, the God of Abraham, the God of Isaac and the God of Jacob." At this, Moses hid his face, because he was afraid to look at God. Exodus 3:1-5 NKJV

The Call of Moses came as a result of desperate cry of the children of Israel in bondage for deliverance:

> The LORD said, "I have indeed seen the misery of my people in Egypt. I have heard them crying out because of their slave drivers, and I am concerned about their suffering. So I have come down to rescue them from the hand of the Egyptians and to bring them up out of that land into a good and spacious land, a land flowing with milk and honey—the home of the Canaanites, Hittites, Amorites, Perizzites, Hivites and Jebusites. And now the cry of the Israelites has reached me, and I have seen the way the Egyptians are oppressing them. So now, go. I am sending you to Pharaoh to bring my people the Israelites out of Egypt.
> Exodus 3:7-10 NKJV.

Although, the birth of Moses was by divine orchestration, the events surrounding his call were all divinely arranged by God to get him to receive the call. But the hallmark of all of these events was the calling, and his assignment.

The Calling of the Lord always leads to divine assignment. These areas have been well taught in my previous books: "Journey of Faith", & "Destined for Greatness".

The assignment God gave Moses was to get His people out of Egypt, the land of bondage, so they can worship and serve God. I believe the gospel today should be about the birth, the death, the resurrection, the ascension, and the coming of Jesus Christ. This is what every Christian Ministries should be about. The overview of every call is to proclaim and explain the gospel of our Lord Jesus Christ and set people free from the bondage of Satan, disciple the saints to be followers of Christ, and to release the saints into various ministries in fulfillment of their callings. Anything short of these is no Ministry of Jesus Christ.

Moses understood his call, he stuck to it, God was with him, and he delivered. If we must continue to see the power of God working wonders in our lives and ministries, we had better be doing what we've been called to do.

What Is Your Vision? It all starts with a vision for your calling. What is your vision? You can't go into ministry without having a vision for the ministry. You can't be in leadership with no adequate vision for your position. There must be a mental picture of what you see tomorrow, from where you are today. This is in agreement with Dr. Gregory Morris:

> At the very core of leadership is vision. One of the greatest tragedies in Christian leadership is when leaders have no vision of the future. And if vision is not in the heart of the leaders, it certainly will not be in their followers.[6]

Everyone called into ministry or leadership must first possess a vision for where they are heading before they are qualified to lead others. Otherwise it will be the blind leading the blind. The chaos in our economy, society, organization, churches is as a result of visionless leaders.

God called Ezekiel with a Prophetic mantle upon his life. And he was given a vision of what God's plan was for the nation of Israel. He was to prophesy (minister) according to what he was told. Take a look at this Scripture:

The hand of the LORD was on me, and he brought me out by the Spirit of the LORD and set me in the middle of a valley; it was full of bones. He led me back and forth among them, and I saw a great many bones on the floor of the valley, bones that were very dry. He asked me, "Son of man, can these bones live?" I said, "Sovereign LORD, you alone know." Then he said to me, "Prophesy to these bones and say to them, 'Dry bones, hear the word of the LORD! This is what the Sovereign LORD says to these bones: I will make breath enter you, and you will come to life. I will attach tendons to you and make flesh come upon you and cover you with skin; I will put breath in you, and you will come to life. Then you will know that I am the LORD.'" So I prophesied as I was commanded. And as I was prophesying, there was a noise, a rattling sound, and the bones came together, bone to bone. I looked, and tendons and flesh appeared on them and skin covered them, but there was no breath in them. Then he said to me, "Prophesy to the breath; prophesy, son of man, and say to it, 'This is what the Sovereign LORD says: Come, breath, from the four winds and breathe into these slain, that they

may live.'" So I prophesied as he commanded me, and breath entered them; they came to life and stood up on their feet—a vast army. Then he said to me: "Son of man, these bones are the people of Israel. They say, 'Our bones are dried up and our hope is gone; we are cut off.' Therefore prophesy and say to them: 'This is what the Sovereign LORD says: My people, I am going to open your graves and bring you up from them; I will bring you back to the land of Israel. Then you, my people, will know that I am the LORD, when I open your graves and bring you up from them. I will put my Spirit in you and you will live, and I will settle you in your own land. Then you will know that I the LORD have spoken, and I have done it, declares the LORD.'"
Ezekiel 37:1-11 NKJV.

Prophet Ezekiel was called by the Lord and was given a vision of the situation, and was told how to deal with the situation.

It all starts with the call, then the vision, following by the third phase, which is the strategy:

Divine Pattern: No two visions are the same. Although, we might all have the same goal which is to reach the world for Christ, but the method, strategy in carrying out the commission might be different. This is where many have missed the move of God in their lives and ministry because we try to pattern ourselves after others. We are uniquely made, our callings are unique, our assignments are unique, so we must stick to the pattern God has for us.

God always gives details on how to carry out His project. He never leaves us in the dark. He did not call us to fail. He wants us to succeed in whatever He commissions us to do. But the key to success in ministry or leadership is knowing and sticking to Divine Blueprint.

"And let them make me a sanctuary, that I may dwell among them. According to all that I show you, that is, the pattern of the tabernacle and the pattern of all its furnishings, just so you shall make it."
Exodus 25:8-9 NKJV.

Your ministry, leadership must be done according to what has been revealed to you. I one time observed a brother who was struggling so badly in his ministry. Now, this kind of hardship was as a result of being outside of God's will not wilderness experience within God's will. After examining his situation, I discovered that he wasn't actually called to Pastor a church. He had an awesome grace for ministry but not as a Pastor. His senior pastor called him and ordained him as a Pastor, released him to go pastor another church. It was a major struggle. Eventually he packed up the ministry.

We have too many who never took time to understand the blueprint for their ministry. One of the trends I have noticed is that, most Christians called or not, wants to own a church. It seems to me that the only way they think you will gain prestige is to be a Pastor or a founder of a church even when you are not called for that. That is dangerous, because, it will eventually lead to abuse in the ministry.

At one time in my life I tried to go get a multi-million dollar building for the church where I was the Senior Pastor, because I was pressurized. The church was growing real fast, other pastors were getting magnificent buildings. It was very tempting. I had people who were ready to finance the project. But after much seeking of God's will and plan, I discovered He wasn't leading me in that direction. Some of the people were disappointed. In their hearts, they wanted competition with other churches, but God has not called me to compete, but to compliment in the Body of Christ. Not too long after that, some of the people whom I thought would have finance the building project left our ministry. Now, if I had made the mistake of buying what God did not authorize, I would have been in serious problems by now.

Some of the troubles we go through in the ministry are as a result of not following the divine blueprint.

God doesn't want you run in the dark. Hear what He said: *"Call to me and I will answer you and tell you great and unsearchable things you do not know."* Jeremiah 33:3.

This principle of following Divine Blueprint was the secret to Jesus' success in ministry:

> "Jesus gave them this answer: "Very truly I tell you, the Son can do nothing by himself; he can do only what he sees his Father doing, because whatever the Father does the Son also does. For the Father loves the Son and shows him all he does. Yes, and he will show him even greater works than these, so that you

will be amazed." John 5:19-20 NKJV

Jesus revealed the key to success by what He said in the above text. Are you leading according to God's pattern? Are you building according to the pattern that was revealed to you? Are you trying to please people or compete with others? Today, God has you reading this book because He wants to deliver you and restore you back to His perfect will for you. One thing you need to realize is that nobody can beat you being you.

CHAPTER TWO

LEADERSHIP TRAINING

Nobody starts at the finish line. Every superstar, great men and women we admire today all had a beginning. It's one thing to have a vision, and know what your calling is. It is another to understand that there is a process to getting there. Miracles happen when preparation meets opportunity.

I emphasized on this a lot in my other book, "Destined for Greatness".

When God calls, He also equips you for that assignment He has for you. You will never be greater than what you have in the inside of you. No organization, church will grow past the leaders. Show me an organization, or group, making impact in the world, I will show you a great leader behind the great move. What's so sad today is that we have too many aspiring to be great leaders yet they don't want to pay the price. Remember, success comes with a price.

The kind of assignment God has for you will determine the kind of training He will recommend for you. In this chapter we will examine two groups of people you need in your life, if you're going to be the great leader God wants for you. Every great spiritual leader you find today had one time in their lives gone through these phases of training I am about to share. For some of you reading this book, you will come to understand where you are in your preparation stage in your journey to leadership, and why God placed you where you are right now.

There are two groups of people you must meet if you will excel in your leadership. The first group is that of King Saul. You will be likened to David under Saul. You must learn all you can from Saul, because he has a lot to teach you on how leadership should not be done.

The second group of people will be that of Apostle Paul. Apostle Paul on the other hand is the mentor that will help you develop you gift, challenge your potential, and place you on the platform of success.

It is imperative that you meet both groups. Otherwise you will not have a balanced leadership mentality. It is also crucial you meet King Saul first before Apostle Paul in other for you to appreciate every level of success God will eventually give you.

Let's break it down:

1. Leadership Training 101

The story of King Saul and David isn't a fairy tale in Christianity. The Bible is full of lessons we have learnt, taught from the reign and leadership of both Saul and David. But there are key lessons we need to employ to buttress our teaching in this subject. If you will ever be great in life, you must go through your training under King Saul.

David was just a shepherd boy whom God chose before he himself realized that he was the chosen one. He was busy with the assignment of taking care of the sheep of his father. A man who could take care of the sheep can definitely take care of God's people. You need to realize that sheep was always used in Scripture to symbolize God's children because of the nature of the animal. While David was busy tending for his father, Jesse' sheep, protecting them from the lions, wolves, God saw the King he would become in him. His past was his preparation 101. Little did he know that it was going to lead to his elevation eventually: *"Your servant used to keep his father's sheep, and when a lion or a bear came and took a lamb out of the flock, I went out after it and struck it, and delivered the lamb from its mouth; and when it arose against me, I caught it by its beard, and struck and killed it."* 1 Samuel 17:34-35 NKJV.

Too many people complain of their past. Blame their history for their present predicament. The truth is every great person in life must have a past. Your history is the pre-requisite you need to enroll into the school of Spiritual leadership. Your past can usher you into future success if you know what to do with it. Stop complaining of what happened yesterday. Start applying the principles you have learnt from yesterday's failures for today's success. This was exactly what David did that promoted him:

> So Saul clothed David with his armor, and he put a bronze helmet on his head; he also clothed him with a coat of mail. David fastened his sword to his armor and tried to walk, for he had not tested them. And David said to Saul, "I cannot walk with these, for I have not tested them." So David took them off. Then he took his staff in his hand; and he chose for himself five smooth stones from the brook, and put them in a shepherd's bag, in a pouch which he had, and his sling was in his hand. And he drew near to the Philistine. So the Philistine came, and began

drawing near to David, and the man who bore the shield went before him. And when the Philistine looked about and saw David, he disdained him; for he was only a youth, ruddy and good-looking. So the Philistine said to David, "Am I a dog that you come to me with sticks?" And the Philistine cursed David by his gods. And the Philistine said to David, "Come to me, and I will give your flesh to the birds of the air and the beasts of the field!"

Then David said to the Philistine, "You come to me with a sword, with a spear, and with a javelin. But I come to you in the name of the LORD of hosts, the God of the armies of Israel, whom you have defied. This day the LORD will deliver you into my hand, and I will strike you and take your head from you. And this day I will give the carcasses of the camp of the Philistines to the birds of the air and the wild beasts of the earth, that all the earth may know that there is a God in Israel. Then all this assembly shall know that the LORD does not save with sword and spear; for the battle is the LORD's, and He will give you into our hands." So it was, when the Philistine arose and came and drew near to meet David, that David hurried and ran toward the army to meet the

Philistine. Then David put his hand in his bag and took out a stone; and he slung it and struck the Philistine in his forehead, so that the stone sank into his forehead, and he fell on his face to the earth.

So David prevailed over the Philistine with a sling and a stone, and struck the Philistine and killed him. But there was no sword in the hand of David. Therefore David ran and stood over the Philistine, took his sword and drew it out of its sheath and killed him, and cut off his head with it.

1 Samuel 17:38-51 NKJV.

David used what he knew how to use best, his shepherd's sling and stones for battle rather than Saul's armor. This is one big lesson every leader must learn. ***"You cannot run with somebody else's revelation."*** What was not revealed to you cannot work for you in the long haul. It might work for a short while, eventually it will fizzle out.

We have preachers today who try to preach other peoples' messages. Some try to sound, and act like others. We must learn from David. He chose to stick to what he knew was for him. He depended on yesterday's testimony for today's victory, not the failures. David also understood the divine moment. He knew this was his moment God had been preparing him all this while. And He seized the divine moment. Understanding spiritual timing in your assignment is the compass that will lead to great success. God has a time and season for whoever He wants to use. Remember, David was already ordained before now (1 Samuel 16:12-13), but he had to wait for God to announce him. God will announce you if you wait for him. Although you have a calling, unusual anointing, grace, etc. But, wait on God so you don't abort your vision.

2. Leadership Training 102

David had to learn after God had given him victory, that "Success is offensive". Everyone who desires leadership must know that you will offend people if you going to be successful. There are people out there who will dislike you for what you have achieved, for the grace of God upon you, for the spiritual gifts you possess; the anointing God has given you, your intelligence. Just like David.

So David went out wherever Saul sent him, and behaved wisely. And Saul set him over the men of war, and he was accepted in the sight of all the people and also in the sight of Saul's servants. Now it had happened as they were coming home, when David was returning from the slaughter of the Philistine, that the women had come out of all the cities of Israel, singing and dancing, to meet King Saul, with tambourines, with joy, and with musical instruments. So the women sang as they danced, and said:

"Saul has slain his thousands, And David his ten thousands." Then Saul was very angry, and the saying displeased him; and he said, "They have ascribed to David ten thousands, and to me they have ascribed only thousands. Now what more can he have but the kingdom?" **So Saul eyed David from that day forward.** And it happened on the next day that the distressing spirit from God came upon Saul, and he prophesied inside the house. So David played music with his hand, as at other times; but there was a spear in Saul's hand. And Saul cast the spear, for he said, "I will pin David to the wall!" But David escaped his presence twice. Now Saul

was afraid of David, because the LORD was with him, but had departed from Saul. Therefore Saul removed him from his presence, and made him his captain over a thousand; and he went out and came in before the people. And David behaved wisely in all his ways, and the LORD was with him.
1 Samuel 18:1-14 NKJV.

The reason why King Saul disliked David was because success was ascribed to him. And he thought within himself that, this same David will one day become King. He didn't like that.

There was a reason why God allowed David to serve under King Saul. Though God knew that Saul will try to kill him, yet David was placed under Saul's leadership. And ultimately under the sovereign protective hand of God. David had to learn humility. You don't know what it means to be humble until you've been lifted. I hear people talk about how humble they are, based on their physical appearances, the kind of clothes they wear, the house they live, the title they bear, etc. It's so funny how we today use material, physical things as yardstick to qualify spiritual fruits. You can have rags on and still be proud. You can be a nobody and still be proud. **Humility is a spiritual fruit.**

It is character based. It comes from within, not from the outward. God develops you in humility by placing you in a situation where you must come to realize that without him you are nothing. This is true humility. Humility is acknowledging that God, and He alone is your source, sustainer, and your goal. When this is inbuilt within you, it will be easy to submit to people, work with others. Because you know it's not about them but about God. Such was the case of David. God was maturing his character through King Saul.

Until you come in contact with Saul, you are not ready for the throne. King Saul is a 'type' for jealousy, envy, and bitterness in leadership. This is common within churches. Many upcoming spiritual leaders, ministers, pastors, have questioned me in this regard in some of my leadership seminars and teachings, on why they feel rejected, slammed, by those above them. I often tell them, it's the route to success in ministry. Those, especially with prophetic gifts, called into the prophetic office often face persecution when serving under a Pastor who doesn't have a prophetic or apostolic mantle. The Prophet is into the supernatural and power manifestation, while the pastor loves to teach and preach God's word, and might not necessarily demonstrate spiritual gifts. But today's world is about power demonstration. Therefore, the Prophet has every tendency to draw attention to himself, if he is not matured, and will have problems with the Pastor of the church where he serves. This was a typical scenario of David and King Saul. I also experienced this coming up as a minister with a prophetic call on my life. I had couple of experiences where some of those I looked up to turning against me. If not for my personal encounter of who God is, I would have left the ministry. But thank God today, those experiences have helped me to raise other ministers without getting jealous of their gifts, callings, or how big their ministries might turn out.

Did you notice that David never had such experience with his leaders he mentored when he became King? God taught David how not to rule through the leadership of Saul.

Jesus himself had to experience the kiss of Judas, betrayed by His very own disciple, Judas for him to get to the throne. *"Now His betrayer had given them a signal, saying, "Whomever I kiss, He is the One; seize Him and lead Him away safely"* Mark 14:43 NKJV.

Don't quit ministry, your leadership because of whatever persecution you are going through. It is part of the process. You learn some rudiments for successful ministry, sometimes by learning how not to do it. Sometimes God places you under a leadership, ministry, and organization that will eventually fail. This shouldn't scare you away, but learn all you can from the experience.

3. Leadership Training 103

Now, haven learnt rough leadership through King Saul. You've escaped all the miseries and havocs that these leaders brought to you. You almost thought of quitting, you probably thought you will not be able to trust anyone anymore. You probably have said to yourself, there is too much politics in the church, I am not sure if ministry is for me. It's okay to think that way. I went through it myself, until I met the next group of people I am about to introduce you to. You have learnt under King Saul how not to lead, you need to meet the right mentor(s) that will teach you how ministry should be done.

This group is what I likened to Apostle Paul. There is a big difference between King Saul and Apostle Paul. King Saul was busy about building and protecting his own Kingdom.

That was why he was so jealous of David. Thinking he was going to lose it, which he eventually did (1 Samuel 31:6).

Apostle Paul was busy with God's Kingdom. He was passionate about taking the gospel to the uttermost part of the world. He knew he can't do it alone. A true apostle indeed, he empowered others the same way God empowered him. He entrusted to others what God gave to him. **He knew that the key to Kingdom expansion is the law of multiplication.** He knew he was not a success if he had no successor. Hear what Apostle Paul said to his spiritual son, Timothy:

"Therefore I remind you to stir up the gift of God which is in you through the laying on of my hands. For God has not given us a spirit of fear, but of power and of love and of a sound mind" 2 Timothy 1;6-7 NKJV.

Apostle Paul ordained the young Timothy into the ministry, committed the work of pastoring in Ephesus into his hands. He imparted grace into him, and counseled him to continue to 'stir' up the spiritual gifts inside of him, and not to be afraid of the oppositions and persecutions around him.

Scholars have said that Timothy was about nineteen years of age when he started pastoring. The church in Ephesus was a mega church in Asia Minor. Ephesus was known for her Greek mythology, and Gnostic teachings were prevalent in those days. It was a huge spiritual battle. At this time Apostle Paul had already planted the seed of the gospel in that land, and was in prison. So he commissioned Timothy to continue the work. Hear what he further said:

> You therefore, my son, be strong in the grace that is in Christ Jesus. And the things that you have heard from me among many witnesses, commit these to faithful men who will be able to teach others also. You therefore must endure hardship as a good soldier of Jesus Christ. No one engaged in warfare entangles himself with the affairs of this life, that he may please him who enlisted him as a soldier. And also if anyone competes in athletics, he is not crowned unless he competes according to the rules. The hardworking farmer must be first to partake of the crops. Consider what I say, and may the Lord give you understanding in all things.
> Remember that Jesus Christ, of the seed of David, was raised from the dead according to my gospel, for which I suffer trouble as an evildoer, even to the point of chains; but the word of God is not chained. Therefore I endure all things for the sake of the

elect, that they also may obtain the salvation which is in Christ Jesus with eternal glory. This is a faithful saying: For if we died with Him, We shall also live with Him. If we endure, We shall also reign with Him. If we deny Him, He also will deny us. If we are faithless, He remains faithful; He cannot deny Himself.

Remind them of these things, charging them before the Lord not to strive about words to no profit, to the ruin of the hearers. Be diligent to present yourself approved to God, a worker who does not need to be ashamed, rightly dividing the word of truth. But shun profane and idle babblings, for they will increase to more ungodliness. And their message will spread like cancer. Hymenaeus and Philetus are of this sort, who have strayed concerning the truth, saying that the resurrection is already past; and they overthrow the faith of some. Nevertheless the solid foundation of God stands, having this seal: "The Lord knows those who are His," and, "Let everyone who names the name of Christ depart from iniquity." But in a great house there are not only vessels of gold and silver, but also of wood and clay, some for honor and some for dishonor. Therefore if anyone cleanses himself from the latter, he will be a vessel for honor, sanctified and useful for the Master, prepared for every good work. Flee also youthful lusts; but pursue righteousness, faith, love, peace with those who call on the Lord out of a pure heart. But avoid foolish and ignorant disputes, knowing that they generate strife. And a servant of the Lord must not quarrel but be gentle to all, able to teach, patient, in humility correcting those who are in opposition, if God perhaps will grant them repentance, so that they may know the truth, and that they may come to their senses and escape the snare of the devil, having been taken captive by him to do his will.

2 Timothy 2:1-26 NKJV

Apostle Paul did not only give Timothy the heart of the gospel of Jesus Christ, he also gave him the blueprint for solid leadership, as a minister of the gospel. According to Craig Keener, *"Rabbis stressed the passing on of traditions from one generation to the next generation, noting that the process had begun long before them. They usually emphasized the views of the founder more than those of immediate predecessors."*[7]

Apostle Paul passed the gospel, and principles he had received, learnt over time to Timothy, with the understanding that, the Kingdom of God must continue.

Today's generation of spiritual leaders are going through one of the toughest challenges in ministry the world has ever witnessed with the rapid growth of social change. Most leaders today were not fully prepared for the challenge of the 21st century ministry or leadership. Getting formal degrees is one thing, but receiving impartation and grace from fathers and mothers in the faith is another.

One time I did a research on a nation's spiritual leaders. And I discovered that the young, upcoming leaders in ministry were stepping out in ministry on their own, starting up churches without being ordained, doing great works for the Lord without any form of accountability. I was concerned, but later I discovered that there were too many bullies as fathers in the faith in that country. Many mentors spiritually abused their protégés, they never want to see young ministers rise to prominence. They feel threatened when a young minister with mighty grace is in the spotlight. Does this sound like King Saul? And we wonder why we have so many spiritual vagabonds in the ministry? We wonder why the gospel has been corrupted so much in our generation. God is calling spiritual leaders to repentance. One thing we must constantly remember is that someone's blood was shed for this gospel we preach and teach. That blood wasn't just any other; it was precious, adored, and great. He is the Son of the Living God. His name is Jesus, and He is the Christ.

One time, I asked one of my spiritual fathers whom I admire his success greatly, what is his secret of his success? He replied me in one sentence: *"Make other people successful, You will be successful"*. Wow! That is the principle of multiplication. That is what the Kingdom of God should be all about.

CHAPTER THREE

CHOOSING BETWEEN TRADITION OR RELEVANCE

This is one of the most crucial and sensitive subject to be discussed. It affects everything we do. It shapes our mindset, gives us our worldview. Through research, I have discovered that every generation goes through this dilemma of wanting their leaders to be able to relate to current issues. And the leaders struggle either to be relevant or stick with traditions. I must stress here that we will streamline this teaching to the context of leadership, God's way, which this book is all about. That way we don't digress so much, since, the subject of 'Tradition' is a broad one.

Tradition is simply a practice, custom, stories that are adhered by some group of people and have been passed down from generation to generation. Jesus in His days had to deal with the traditions of the day as opposed to relevancy. Let's learn from Jesus, the greatest spiritual leader ever lived.

> Do not think that I came to destroy the Law or the Prophets. I did not come to destroy but to fulfill. For assuredly, I say to you, till heaven and earth pass away, one jot or one tittle will by no means pass from the law till all is fulfilled. Whoever therefore breaks one of the least of these commandments, and teaches men so, shall be called least in the kingdom of heaven; but whoever does and teaches them, he shall be called great in the kingdom of heaven. For I say to you, that unless your righteousness exceeds the righteousness of the scribes and Pharisees, you will by no means enter the kingdom of heaven. Matthew 5:17-20 NKJV.

Jesus had a lot of oppositions from the Pharisees of his day. The Pharisees were regarded as the custodian of the law. They were traditional in their approach. They, in fact held on to oral tradition more than the Word of God.

The Pharisees were so blind to their ways and practices that they missed their own salvation. Although, they thought they kept God's Word, but they definitely lacked the understanding of the Word of God that was passed on to them.

Jesus, to them was a rebel to God's Word, to the traditions they held on for years so dearly. They knew Jesus' story. How can He come and overturn what has been held in high esteem for generations? This was a big issue then, and is still an issue today with different people, churches, and leaders.

Jesus made it emphatically clear that His mission wasn't to destroy the Law (message) that had been passed down to them, but to fulfill them. Which means Jesus brought the correlation between theory and practice, from history to relevance. He stressed that until the people's perspective change about the righteousness of God, they will be denied access into Heaven. The Pharisees worldview of righteousness was outward appearances, outward cleansing, and works. This eventually leads to pretense and falsehood. But the righteousness Jesus taught came from within as a result of sincere salvation, and the Holy Spirit transforming oneself from the inside out. The Pharisees were more concerned of the natural, while Jesus focused on the spiritual as the basis, which eventually affects the natural man. These were conflicts of worldviews.

Today, our worldviews shapes our Leadership, Organizations, and Ministries. It affects everything we do. The outcry of many out there is that, why is the church not relevant to the people and the issues of the day. Why are the sermons not transforming people? Have you noticed that churches, ministries, small groups, Para-church groups, spring up by the minute in America, yet our nation is still in so much darkness?

Landa Cope buttresses this in the research done by a British journalist which she wrote:

> A British journalist who was saying that Christians believe that many of them living in a community will affect that community for good. The greater the Christian presence, the greater the benefit to the society at large. He went on to look at the most Christianized city in America to see how this influence works out practically. Dallas, Texas was the most Christianized city in America at that time. Churches abound in Dallas and a large number boast full pews. The TV host looked at the statistics and information you would be concerned about if you were going to raise your children in a community. Will my children be safe on the streets? Can they get a respectable, safe education? Will I be able to house, clothe and feed my family? Will my children have blatant exposure to drugs and other destructive influences? Are the police equally

interested in our protection, and is these entire true regardless of my color, nationality or creed?

By the time my English host was done with the Dallas study I was devastated. No one would want to live in a city in that condition. The crime, the decrepit social systems, the disease, the economic discrepancies, the racial injustice. And this was the "most Christianized" city in America.

The host took this devastating picture of a broken community to the Christian leaders and asked for their observations. He chose leaders of status and integrity. With simplicity, the narrator asked each minister, "As a Christian leader, what is your response to the condition of your community?" Without exception, in various ways, they all said the same thing, "This is not my concern... I'm a spiritual leader."[8]

Well, the report spoke a lot. But we must establish here that the ministry of Jesus Christ affected humanity in all ramifications both while He was on earth and till present. He wasn't tied to the status quo, He was a revolutionary spiritual leader. His ministry was felt on the streets, homes, government, religious circles, etc.

Now it happened, as He went into the house of one of the rulers of the Pharisees to eat bread on the Sabbath, that they watched Him closely. And behold, there was a certain man before Him who had dropsy. And Jesus, answering, spoke to the lawyers and Pharisees, saying, "Is it lawful to heal on the Sabbath?" But they kept silent. And He took him and healed him, and let him go. Then He answered them, saying, "Which of you, having a donkey or an ox that has fallen into a pit, will not immediately pull him out on the Sabbath day?" And they could not answer Him regarding these things. Luke 14:1-6 NKJV.

Jesus healed people on the Sabbath day which was unlawful to the Pharisees, the religious sect. The Pharisees symbolizes, in our day, the system that has crippled the church, held back the anointing as a result of erroneous belief, ungodly traditions, denominational rules and regulations. But now is the time, God is calling His Church to break out free from whatever that has held her back. You, as leader must set your mind free. God cannot be put in a box. Leaders must learn to be flexible, God is not predictable, and He is not one you can figure out His equation. We just have to be ready for whatever direction He wants to take us.

One time, God told me to take our Sunday morning service to the street for evangelism. That morning, our service was evangelism on the street, people's homes. That day, I saw members of the Church functioning in their ministry that baffled me. Literally, members prayed for the sick, leading people to Christ. I was amazed. God moved, and the impact of our ministry is still being felt in that city. The mindset of our church members in that city is beyond just sitting in the pews. We have exposed them to real ministry; members see themselves as ministers wherever they find themselves. This was an eye opener to me then into the apostolic ministry I am involved in today.

Would you break out of every ungodly tradition that has held you back? I must strike the balance here that not all traditions should be eradicated. A tradition within the frame of biblical worldview that affects humanity is definitely something to keep. Remember, Traditions could translate into values that uphold human life. My main thrust in this chapter is the issue of being relevant to issues of the day. Ministry is about the people, not necessarily organizational creed.

PART THREE

PEOPLE'S MANAGEMENT

Then the LORD spoke to Moses, saying: "See, I have called by name Bezalel the son of Uri, the son of Hur, of the tribe of Judah. And I have filled him with the Spirit of God, in wisdom, in understanding, in knowledge, and in all manner of workmanship, to design artistic works, to work in gold, in silver, in bronze, in cutting jewels for setting, in carving wood, and to work in all manner of workmanship. "And I, indeed I, have appointed with him Aholiab the son of Ahisamach, of the tribe of Dan; and I have put wisdom in the hearts of all the gifted artisans, that they may make all that I have commanded you.
Exodus 31: 1-6

CHAPTER ONE

DIVINE HELPERS

Two major areas of concern that comes to mind when God gives you an assignment, or calls you into the ministry:
1. How do I get money to carry out the assignment?
2. Who will help me?

These are questions that run through the mind of the average visionary. Laying emphasis on the Scripture quoted in the opening (Exodus 31:1-6). God gave Moses the vision to build the Tabernacle, He also sent the men with skill and wealth to help him with the building of the vision. Whenever, God gives an assignment, He also makes provision for that assignment, including the financial resources. It might not come immediately, but will eventually surface as you progress with the assignment, doing it His way. Before He calls, He takes care of all the basics that you will need to fulfill destiny. Cast the vision, and leave the others to Him.

In this chapter, we will learn how God connects people to us, and subsequently, how to manage this people. I have seen situations where visionaries don't understand their positions in the vision and dealing with the helpers of the vision. When a visionary is displaced, it brings disarray to the whole vision. I have seen situations where people with money, financing the vision, try to give directions to how the vision should be run. Just like a tither in the church telling the Pastor how the church should be run. This is one major problem almost every pastor I have come across, deals with or have dealt with.

First, let's deal with the 2 groups of people God sends to you, when he gives you the vision. I believe every establishment, whether secular or spiritual needs this people to run any organization:

1.   **Skillful People**:

God knows that it takes some specific skill to build the Tabernacle, which of course, Moses didn't have. That was why He called skillful men alongside with him. One of the ways you know God indeed has called you into assignment is that you will discover that the vision is beyond your abilities. It will be overwhelming. It will take God and the right people to help you accomplish it.

It's amazing, seeing people who are not gifted in an area trying so hard in order to be noticed. Those who are skillful, gifted in what they do, don't struggle in doing what they know how to do best. Wake them up in the morning, they will still function. You are not gifted if you need to go through school to learn what you do. I have heard of some Ministers say they had to go through Seminary to become Pastors. "You don't go through to become somebody". You are already whom God has made you to be. He gifted you before you born (Jeremiah 1:5). You go through training to improve on your gifts, refine your gifts, and learn how to implement what is already given. Spiritual gifts, talents is not acquired, it is given.

Every divine assignment needs this kind of people who have been gifted in the area of your calling. As a leader, after you've discovered what your assignment is, then you need to start praying and calling forth all the skillful people God has ordained for that assignment. People that you need to help you. They are already placed spiritually, but you need to call them forth. Let them manifest.

Like I mentioned earlier on, they don't struggle in what they do. They love what they do. I must say here that some have corrupted their gifts with money. They tend to put money first before using what God endowed them with. Well, for some, they were abused. People took advantage over them. Others are just corrupted.

Well as a spiritual leader, when skillful people come to you. Let them see themselves as volunteers first, until the organization possesses enough money to pay them. I would advise that you compensate them, no matter how little or in giving some kind of material gifts. But you must let them know that they are only being appreciated and compensated not paid. These are two different things: To be paid as one hired, and to be compensated for rendering service. Servant hood has to be the watchword from the onset; otherwise you will struggle with it eventually as the ministry grows bigger. I learnt this from a horrible experience. Because sometimes when God sends skillful people to you, if you don't apply caution, you will go out of your way to keep them. Sometimes, some of this people will prey on that. Well if I leave, nobody will do it is always their mentality. I have experience this a lot in the ministry. Some left me, but after I learnt that the vision is not mine, it is God's. I am only a caretaker. Then, fear was cast out, because God is faithful enough to take care of what is His.

In conclusion of this, you must understand that spiritual gifts are given, not acquired or earned.

2. Loyal People:

While skillful, gifted people can help the vision move faster. It will make others identify with the vision God has given you. You also need loyal people around you. This set of people might not have the necessary skill you need at the moment, but you need them if your establishment is going to stand the test of time ahead.

This people are people of integrity. Integrity is from the heart, it cannot be taught. It comes from regeneration of the Holy Spirit. Most times this kind of people are often hard to find. God has to connect them to you. So hold on to them. I must stress here that some can be both loyal and skillful. What I mean by this is that they have spiritual gifts, as well as spiritual fruits. This is the best thing that can happen to any establishment. Because spiritual gifts are given, but spiritual fruits are cultivated. You cannot pray and impart the fruit of humility, patience, gentleness, etc., on anyone. You can only pray that God help them to become all of that. God answers such prayers by cultivation from the inside out.

One time I had a situation where there was a conflict between one of my skillful workers who possessed very little spiritual fruit but highly gifted and another loyal worker, who was very faithful, full of integrity, excellent worker, gifted, but not as announced like the other. I was in a situation where I had to let one go, because it was going to eventually affect the whole ministry. After much prayer, I was led by the Spirit to let the Skillful one go. This might sound absurd, because the skillful worker was highly productive. Do you know my decision paid off in the long run?

Loyal people, with spiritual fruits are hard to find in today's world. You will always find gifted people, but majority have little or no spiritual fruits. You must learn how to apply discernment as a leader.

CHAPTER TWO

LEADERSHIP EMPOWERMENT

The quickest way to build or destroy an organization is through the leaders. Everyone God assigns to you is important. If they are not important to your vision or assignment, God will not send them. The onus rests on the overall leader to discover the ability, grace, anointing, each one in the group has and how they can implement on the overall vision.

Dr. R.T Kendall, a re-known scholar in the area of the anointing has this to say: "Everybody has an anointing. The apostle Paul called it "gifts" in 1 Corinthians 12:4-11. The Greek word charismata really means grace- gift." [9]

> Some anointing, then, have a high profile like the eye or the head. Some anointing has a lower profile like the hands or the feet. "The eye cannot say to the hand, "I don't need you! And the head cannot say to the feet, 'I don't need you! On the contrary, those parts of the body that seem to be weaker are indispensable."1 Corinthians 12:21-22

> Some people have an anointing with no apparent profile at all, like the kidneys or intestines, which are indispensable. God's design is that there should be 'no division in the body, but that its parts should have equal concern for each other'.[10]

Sometimes I hear comments of leaders of churches, after much complain about the overall leader of the church. They tend to withdraw their commitments and duties towards the development of the vision. They mostly say, after all, it is the Pastor's church. Therefore, it's none of our business if things don't work right, or if the vision collapses. This is as a result of not seeing themselves in the picture.

For every vision to be successful, everyone, especially those in the leadership must see themselves as a team, which means if it fails, they all fail, not just the visionary but everyone connected to the vision. You can always tell when leaders are committed to a vision by the amount of time they put in, the resources they invest into it. Only a myopic person will invest their time and resources into something they are not sure of its destination.

Every visionary has the obligation to cast the vision in such a way that everyone feels they are part of something bigger and greater than themselves. They must sense that connection, they have to have something to hope for, something to die for, something to expect. That is vision.

Most times the danger in leadership is to feel that those beneath you have no adequate training, incapable of handling responsibilities. With that notion, they get relegated, which eventually leads to redundancy. This is where the vision begins to suffer. The best way to keep a vision alive is to give others responsibilities to handle, even when they are incapable at the moment. What sustains you in your leadership position is the level of enablement you give your people. Show me a leader, who empowers his subjects, I will show you a leader who will remain standing for a long time. I have watched leaders suppressed the gifts of others, little did they know that they are only killing their vision. Moses wasn't a success until Joshua rose up to leadership:

Now Amalek came and fought with Israel in Rephidim. And Moses said to Joshua, "Choose us

some men and go out, fight with Amalek. Tomorrow I will stand on the top of the hill with the rod of God in my hand." So Joshua did as Moses said to him, and fought with Amalek. And Moses, Aaron, and Hur went up to the top of the hill. And so it was, when Moses held up his hand, that Israel prevailed; and when he let down his hand, Amalek prevailed. But Moses' hands became heavy; so they took a stone and put it under him, and he sat on it. And Aaron and Hur supported his hands, one on one side, and the other on the other side; and his hands were steady until the going down of the sun. So Joshua defeated Amalek and his people with the edge of the sword.
Exodus 17:8-13 NKJV.

The key to the Israelites victory wasn't because Joshua and his great army were strong enough to conquer the Amalekites. Joshua had learnt combat from Moses, learnt the art of warfare. Now it was time for him to put to work what he had learnt. Moses didn't just push him out there to fail or die. Moses was in the background with his hand lifted up to heaven, which symbolizes intercession. He knew if Joshua fails the children of Israel all fails. This was beyond Joshua. This was about Yahweh, and His will to be done on earth. When Moses' hand grew weary, the others came and supported him.

I really wish that the Body of Christ would grasp this concept of unity, and put every disagreement aside. We are not in competition. After all, it's not about us, but about God and His Kingdom being manifested on earth. It's a privilege to be chosen as a participant in this divine project.

As a visionary, it is important to know that people grow with the level of assignment committed to them. Don't be afraid to give people assignment. The art of leadership is delegation. As you delegate, you must also give room for mistakes. People are not perfect.

This was Jesus' style in leadership training.

> "Then the seventy returned with joy, saying, "Lord, even the demons are subject to us in Your name." And He said to them, "I saw Satan fall like lightning from heaven. Behold, I give you the authority to trample on serpents and scorpions, and over all the power of the enemy, and nothing shall by any means hurt you. Nevertheless do not rejoice in this, that the spirits are subject to you, but rather rejoice because your names are written in heaven. Luke 10:17-20 NKJV.

One common principle practiced by Jesus in the New Testament was that He always took his disciples with Him on His missions, ministry opportunities. He also gave them opportunities to practice what they learn. When they don't get it right, He corrected them, taught them, and instructed them.

> And when they had come to the multitude, a man came to Him, kneeling down to Him and saying, "Lord, have mercy on my son, for he is an epileptic and suffers severely; for he often falls into the fire and often into the water. So I brought him to Your disciples, but they could not cure him." Then Jesus answered and said, "O faithless and perverse generation, how long shall I be with you? How long shall I bear with you? Bring him here to Me." And Jesus rebuked the demon, and it came out of him; and the child was cured from that very hour. Then the disciples came to Jesus privately and said, "Why could we not cast it out?" So Jesus said to them, "Because of your unbelief; for assuredly, I say to you, if you have faith as a mustard seed, you will say to this mountain, 'Move from here to there,' and it will move; and nothing will be impossible for

you. However, this kind does not go out except by prayer and fasting." Matthew 17:14-21 NKJV.

Jesus never left His disciples helpless, or to figure things out by themselves in their misery. He knew they will need to continue the mission after He is gone. So, He taught them what they needed to know at that moment. **A vision that outlives the visionary is a vision that empowers.**
As a Leader, You must empower others by teaching them and giving them opportunities to exercise their gifts. Some ministries teach their leaders but don't give opportunity for them to exercise their gifts until when they are released out of the local church. They get out on the field trying to figure out where and how to start. Some other ministries give people lots of opportunity without adequate training. In such places you find immaturity, and abuse of power. Most of such places you see flesh at work not the Holy Spirit. There need to be balance in Leadership empowerment.
Jesus took time to invest in the twelve while He was busy with His ministry because of His vision of global harvest. Invest in your leaders and you ministry will be enlarged. You will be amazed how God will use that to increase your ministry. Mentoring is better caught than taught. Don't just

tell them what to do, let them watch you doing it. That is truly apostolic. As you pull others up, God will promote you as well.

CHAPTER THREE

DELEGATION, THE ART OF LEADERSHIP

True Leadership is delegation as we have learnt in the previous chapter. But, it is paramount we take it further in this leadership studies, so we can attain balance in our leadership venture.

I have observed in some Christian organizations, people are given positions, responsibilities, office, as a result of their relationship to those in the senior leadership positions. Some Pastors give members positions in order to keep them from leaving their church. The truth is, God is the Lord of the harvest, and only Him can also sustain the harvest.

The worst thing that can happen to a Pastor is to place the wrong people in the right positions. When people are wrongly placed in a church or organization, it often brings confusion rather than blessing. Take a look at this:

> Again David gathered all the choice men of Israel, thirty thousand. And David arose and went with all the people who were with him from Baale Judah to bring up from there the ark of God, whose name is called by the Name, the LORD of Hosts, who

dwells between the cherubim. So they set the ark of God on a new cart, and brought it out of the house of Abinadab, which was on the hill; and Uzzah and Ahio, the sons of Abinadab, drove the new cart.[b] 4 And they brought it out of the house of Abinadab, which was on the hill, accompanying the ark of God; and Ahio went before the ark. Then David and all the house of Israel played music before the LORD on all kinds of instruments of fir wood, on harps, on stringed instruments, on tambourines, on sistrums, and on cymbals.

And when they came to Nachon's threshing floor, **Uzzah put out his hand to the ark of God and took hold of it, for the oxen stumbled.** Then the anger of the LORD was aroused against Uzzah, and God struck him there for his error; and he died there by the ark of God. And David became angry because of the LORD's outbreak against Uzzah; and he called the name of the place Perez Uzzah to this day. 2 Samuel 6:1-8 NKJV.

One would have thought that Uzzah was doing the right thing by protecting the ark of covenant from stumbling while they were transporting it. But God struck him dead, although he had good intention but he wasn't a Levite, that wasn't his calling. In fact the mode of transportation was all wrong, for God does not ride on animals, but on men. And not just ordinary men, but those He chose. David learnt this in a hard way, and eventually figured out the best way to do it (1 Chron.15:1-2).

This is often our story as well when we try to do God's work in a wrong way; it opens the door for attack. As a spiritual leader, it is your duty to rightly place people. True leadership is delegating responsibility, and giving them the right assignment based on two crucial things: **Spiritual Gifts and Spiritual Fruits.**

People have to be gifted in a certain areas for them to given an area of responsibility. One who is not called and anointed for worship should not be on the worship team.

I have often said that you don't go to seminary to become a Pastor, you have to be called first, then you go through school to receive adequate knowledge and also sharpen your ministerial skills.

The early church understood the implication of placement in the ministry. See what the apostles said:

Now in those days, when the number of the disciples was multiplying, there arose a complaint against the Hebrews by the Hellenists, because their widows were neglected in the daily distribution. Then the twelve summoned the multitude of the disciples and said, **"It is not desirable that we should leave the word of God and serve tables.** Therefore, brethren, seek out from among you seven men of good reputation, full of the Holy Spirit and wisdom, whom we may appoint over this business; but we will give ourselves continually to prayer and to the ministry of the word. Acts 6:1-4

The early apostles spelt it out well. Although there was problems within the congregation, but they decided not to leave their major assignment which was preaching, teaching & prayer. They rather delegate this responsibility to someone who was called, and has the spiritual fruits to handle the position. And Stephen was chosen.

Don't try to do everything by yourself. And stop trying to look for perfect people for the job. When recruiting, one of the ways you know God has His hand on someone for an assignment is:

1. **Passion:** Those called for an assignment always have an overwhelming passion God places in them. It is visible you'll see an unusual passion in that individual concerning the situation. They might keep bringing suggestions to you, when they pray; it will always be their prayer point. If they have resources they will commit it in that direction.
2. **Time:** Time is precious to people, especially those living in the Western world. And they will only spend their quality time doing what they love. They might not have time for any other thing. But they will create time, when they find what they are interested in. This is one area those in leadership must pay close attention to. You want to get the attention of your audience, invest in the area of their interest, even, if that is not your goal. **Always take people from the known to the unknown.**
3. **Resources:** Jesus made this very clear when He said, *"For where your treasure is, there your heart will be also."* Matthew 6:21.

Watch out for the area people spend their money. No one loves to waste money, especially if it is hard earned. One time a Pastor told me how one of his leaders will not support the church financially, but will rather buy musical instruments, sound system for the church. This brother probably is not sure of the accountability of his pastor, but I can tell you he wants the church to succeed and his heart is towards the sound and music of the church. A wise pastor will place such person in the technical department of the church.

Now, besides knowing the gift of the person being placed, you will do good to also watch for the spiritual fruits as well. Just because someone can exhort the church, does not mean such person has enough patience for counseling. Fruits don't hide, it might take some time. But it will eventually surface.

As a leader never be too rigid or to slow to move your workers to a different assignment if they are not bearing fruit. Fruit bearing is mandatory. It is not optional in the Kingdom of God. *"Every tree that does not bear good fruit is cut down and thrown into the fire. Therefore by their fruits you will know them."* Matthew 7:19-20

PART FOUR

ORGANIZATIONAL MANAGEMENT

CHAPTER ONE

ORDERLINESS

Orderliness is one principle that has been too neglected in the things of God. To be disorganized is not to be well positioned for Heavenly, or divine visitation or God's blessings. God wants us to be organized just like He is in Heaven. Disorderliness leads to chaos, and it hinders the move of God.

Too many churches are praying for revival, but their Ministries are not structured, the atmosphere is not right for what they are asking for. Sometimes when the revival comes and the people are not prepared for such move it can eventually destroy rather than bless.

Let us learn from the Prophet Elijah:

> So Ahab sent for all the children of Israel, and gathered the prophets together on Mount Carmel. And Elijah came to all the people, and said, "How long will you falter between two opinions? If the LORD is God, follow Him; but if Baal, follow him." But the people answered him not a word. Then Elijah said to the people, "I alone am left a prophet of the LORD; but Baal's prophets are four

hundred and fifty men. Therefore let them give us two bulls; and let them choose one bull for themselves, cut it in pieces, and lay it on the wood, but put no fire under it; and I will prepare the other bull, and lay it on the wood, but put no fire under it. Then you call on the name of your gods, and I will call on the name of the LORD; and the God who answers by fire, He is God."

So all the people answered and said, "It is well spoken." Now Elijah said to the prophets of Baal, "Choose one bull for yourselves and prepare it first, for you are many; and call on the name of your god, but put no fire under it."

So they took the bull which was given them, and they prepared it, and called on the name of Baal from morning even till noon, saying, "O Baal, hear us!" But there was no voice; no one answered. Then they leaped about the altar which they had made.

And so it was, at noon, that Elijah mocked them and said, "Cry aloud, for he is a god; either he is meditating, or he is busy, or he is on a journey, or perhaps he is sleeping and must be awakened." So they cried aloud, and cut themselves, as was their custom, with knives and lances, until the blood gushed out on them. And when midday was past, they prophesied until the time of the offering of the evening sacrifice. But there was no voice; no one answered, no one paid attention.

Then Elijah said to all the people, "Come near to me." So all the people came near to him. **And he repaired the altar of the LORD that was broken down. And Elijah took twelve stones, according to the number of the tribes of the sons of Jacob, to whom the word of the LORD had come, saying, "Israel shall be your name."** Then with the stones he built an altar in the name of the LORD; and he made a trench around the altar large enough to hold two seahs of seed. And he put the wood in order, cut the bull in pieces, and laid it on the wood, and said, "Fill four waterpots with water, and pour it on the burnt sacrifice and on the wood." Then he said, "Do it a second time," and they did it a second time; and he said, "Do it a third time," and they did it a third time. So the water ran all around the altar; and he also filled the trench with water.

And it came to pass, at the time of the offering of the evening sacrifice, that Elijah the prophet came near and said, "LORD God of Abraham, Isaac, and

Israel, let it be known this day that You are God in Israel and I am Your servant, and that I have done all these things at Your word. Hear me, O LORD, hear me, that this people may know that You are the LORD God, and that You have turned their hearts back to You again."

Then the fire of the LORD fell and consumed the burnt sacrifice, and the wood and the stones and the dust, and it licked up the water that was in the trench. Now when all the people saw it, they fell on their faces; and they said, "The LORD, He is God! The LORD, He is God!" 1 Kings 18:20-39 NKJV

It important to realize, that the children of Israel at this time practiced apostasy. They turned their back from Jehovah and worshipped the god, Baal and Ashtoreth. The leadership at that time led them astray. Only true revival from Jehovah with visible manifestation of God's presence can turn their hearts back. Does this sound familiar? Does it seem like what we have going on today?

Well, Elijah was ordained by God to restore His people back to God. Like we saw in the above Scripture, Elijah didn't just pray for fire of revival to fall. He knew that for there to be revival, there must be restoration. He repaired the broken altar first. He built the altar with 12 stones to commemorate the number of the covenant. He knew Jehovah as a covenant keeping God. He aligned the covenant tie between God and Israel in repairing the altar.

Elijah took time to organize the altar in a way that it was ready for what God was about to release. The sacrifice was then placed on the altar, before he called down fire. Then, Jehovah answered. There was a national revival as a result, and Israel was restored.

I believe Elijah is a "type" of the Church today. We have cried for revival too much without setting our priorities right. Let's repair the broken altars first. Let's restore the church to her proper place in sound doctrine, in worship, in its mission, and nature for which it was created in the first place. We have left the core mission of the church, which is one major reason we don't see the power of God manifesting like we ought to see.

I remember travelling to Costa Rica for a crusade. I visited some of the churches, and what I experienced there was incredible, their worship was full of reverence for God, their hearts were opened and ready for God. The same scenario is what you will see in most of the third world nations. That is why you hear about the unusual move of God, incredible miracles happening in those places. Here in the Western world, we have replaced true worship with entertainment; biblical preaching has been turned into motivational speaking, it's hard to see God move in such an atmosphere. It's all about gratifying the flesh and theology of the mind. We must return back to God and then and only then will we experience God in an impeccable way we long for.

CHAPTER TWO

DIVINE HIERARCHY

Hierarchy In Heaven

When we study the Scriptures, we see that there is orderliness in Heaven. And we are to build according to the pattern in Heaven for the glory of God to be manifested on earth.

God, The Trinity- Ruler of the Heavens. *"Heaven is My throne, And earth is My footstool."* Isaiah 66:1

God is one in three persons: The Father, The Son, & The Holy Spirit. And each personality fulfills His own role in the redemptive plan of God and does not clash. That is why God, The Son in Jesus Christ can stand on earth and call on God, The Father: *"**Father**, I thank You that You have heard Me."* John 11:41b.

Also the same Jesus said to His disciples that His going away will usher in the third person in the trinity, the Holy Spirit: *"Nevertheless I tell you the truth. It is to your advantage that I go away; for if I do not go away, the **Helper** will not come to you; but if I depart, I will send Him to you"* John 16:7

God is one yet separated in functions and don't conflict Himself. As the Father, He oversees His creation. As the Son, He is the redeemer. As the Spirit, He is the sustainer.

The Arc- Angels – Leading Angels: These angels are considered chief angels. They are angels of authority, with a unique assignment. One of their assignments is "heralding the second coming of Christ (1Thess.4:16)".[11]
They lead leagues of angels:

Angel Michael- His name in Hebrew means *"like unto God"*. His assignment is "to protect God's people, the Jews, and to fulfill that which concerns Israel."[12]

This is good to know that we have assigned angels committed to protecting God's own and God's vision. When God calls you and gives you an assignment, you are not by yourself. You have innumerable company of angels assigned to that vision, and they will do whatever it takes to keep it going until it is fulfilled. If you are involved in deliverance or warfare ministry, this is an area to have revelation knowledge as it will help you in signs and wonders. This was what Elisha knew that gave him confidence in the midst of adversity:

Therefore he sent horses and chariots and a great army there, and they came by night and surrounded the city. And when the servant of the man of God arose early and went out, there was an army, surrounding the city with horses and chariots. And his servant said to him, "Alas, my master! What shall we do?"

So he answered, "Do not fear, for those who are with us are more than those who are with them." And Elisha prayed, and said, "Lord, I pray, open his eyes that he may see." Then the Lord opened the eyes of the young man, and he saw. And behold, the mountain was full of horses and chariots of fire all around Elisha. So when the Syrians came down to him, Elisha prayed to the Lord, and said, "Strike this people, I pray, with blindness." And He struck them with blindness according to the word of Elisha. 2 Kings 6:14-18

Angel Gabriel- The Hebrew meaning of Gabriel is *"Man of God"*. Gabriel stands in the presence of God continually. He is considered the angel of Good news. This is because of his access to the very presence of God. He can ascertain God's will for an individual, ministry, organization, or nation. Then he committed to bringing that news. I consider his company of angels as the angels of breakthrough.

> Now in the sixth month **the angel Gabriel** was sent by God to a city of Galilee named Nazareth, to a virgin betrothed to a man whose name was Joseph, of the house of David. The virgin's name was Mary. And having come in, the angel said to her, "Rejoice, highly favored one, the Lord is with you; blessed are you among women!"
> But when she saw him, she was troubled at his saying, and considered what manner of greeting this was. Then the angel said to her, "Do not be afraid, Mary, for you have found favor with God. And behold, you will conceive in your womb and bring forth a Son, and shall call His name Jesus. He will be great, and will be called the Son of the Highest; and the Lord God will give Him the throne of His father David. And He will reign over the house of Jacob forever, and of His kingdom there will be no end. Luke 1:26-33

The Cherubim Angels- These angels are special angels mentioned in the Scriptures as to having unique role. They were asked to protect the tree of life in Gen. 3:23-25. They hover around the mercy seat on the ark of covenant protecting the presence of God, Exodus 25:19-22. They transport God's shekinah glory. In the book of Ezekiel chapter 1, the Prophet gives a vivid description of this set of angels as having 4 faces, 4 wings. They are mighty angels that are unique in their role when it comes to the very presence and glory of God. Despite their 4 different faces of Lion, Man, Eagle, and Ox which symbolizes different assignments in God's agenda, and 4 wings, yet they go one direction without conflict, they fly straight without turning to the left or right. What a mystery!

The Seraphim Angels- The Prophet Isaiah in his writing, chapter 6, describes the Seraphim angels as those who cry out to God all day and night in worship. They proclaim the holiness of God. They are regarded as having six wings which they use for various functions. "Two hiding his face (he could not look at God's glory), two covering his feet (recognizing subservience to the Almighty), and two for flying (taking care of God's business)."[13]

If you understand the role of these angels you will understand why worship is so important in the release of God's presence and power. Their worship is so incredible, *"And the posts of the door moved at the voice of him that cried, and the house was filled with smoke"* Isaiah 6:4. Their worship caused vibration in heaven. I myself witnessed this in one of my heavenly experiences. I heard the Seraphim angels worshipping His holiness, and the voice carried so much power to heal any disease. I wish our churches will worship God to that point that will arouse power for the manifestation of God's glory.

Please note that all through this section, we see that there is orderliness in heaven, from God down to the angels. Each celestial being having its own personality, power, and function. Yet, they all work together for a common goal, all about advancing God's Kingdom.

The Church is to model what happens in heavens and be a replica on earth.

Hierarchy In The Church

For any entity to fulfill its purpose there must be some kind of structure for leadership. Just like it is in heaven, there must be orderliness in the church as well. Let's briefly see what a spiritual church should look like:

Jesus Christ: *"And He is the head of the body, the church, who is the beginning, the firstborn from the dead, that in all things He may have the preeminence."* Colossians 1:18

The above Scripture makes it clear that Jesus Christ is the Head of the Church. He founder Christianity. It is built upon His incarnation, crucifixion, resurrection, and ascension. Without Christ, there is no church (Matt.16:18). So I wonder why men will try to run the church without the head. A body cannot function without the head. The head gives direction to the whole body.

Jesus Christ is the Living Word of God (John 1:1-5). Therefore, the Word of God should serve as a guide for the church of God, not human philosophies or worldly ideas. I have seen Pastors try to apply secular approach for church growth. This eventually turned out to be a social club rather than a spiritual entity. The Word of God is sufficient to run a church if it is well understood and applied.

The Holy Spirit: From the very beginning of creation (Gen.1:1-3), the Holy Spirit has been involved in executing God's will. He is the Divine Executor. The church was born as a result of His coming:

> When the Day of Pentecost had fully come, they were all with one accord in one place. And suddenly there came a sound from heaven, as of a rushing mighty wind, and it filled the whole house where they were sitting. Then there appeared to them divided tongues, as of fire, and one sat upon each of them. And they were all filled with the Holy Spirit and began to speak with other tongues, as the Spirit gave them utterance. Acts 2:1-4

The Holy Spirit gave birth to the Church of Jesus Christ as the executor of God's purpose and plan. And only Him can build and sustain the church. Thank God for all the church growth methodologies we have learnt. If the Holy Spirit is not part of it, it's a waste of time and effort.

Every Pastor must learn how to trust the Word of God, and the Spirit of God to plant, build and sustain the church. The Holy Spirit is called alongside with us to help fulfill divine assignment. To ignore Him or not giving Him his rightful place is tantamount to failure. The reason we have too many dead churches is because the Holy Spirit is not there. He is the life giver.

The Pastor: The Pastor is one called to shepherd God's flock. He is a care taker, an under-shepherd of the Great Shepherd, Jesus Christ, under the direction of the Holy Spirit. The Pastor's primary assignment is to lead and feed God's people. Many Pastors shipwreck their ministries as a result of lack of understanding of their role. Psalm 23 help describes the role of a Shepherd towards the Sheep:

> The LORD is my shepherd; I shall not want. He makes me to lie down in green pastures; He leads me beside the still waters. He restores my soul; He leads me in the paths of righteousness for His name's sake. Yea, though I walk through the valley of the shadow of death, I will fear no evil; For You are with me; Your rod and Your staff, they comfort me. You prepare a table before me in the presence of my enemies; You anoint my head with oil; My cup runs over. Surely goodness and mercy shall follow me all the days of my life; and I will dwell in

the house of the LORD Forever. Psalm 23:1-6

This is the picture of a Shepherd leading and feeding the sheep.

Phillip Keller, in his exposition expounds on the subject of a Shepherd and the Sheep gave some of his insights that the sheep will not lie down until four requirements are met:

1. Owing to their timidity they refuse to lie down unless they are free of all fear.
2. Because of the social behavior within the flock, sheep will not lie down unless they are free from friction with others of their kind.
3. If tormented by flies or parasites, sheep will not lie down. Only when free of these pests can they relax.
4. Sheep will not lie down as long as they feel in need of finding food. They must be free from hunger.[14]

The Pastor's assignment is to make sure the sheep lie down securely in God's presence and enjoy all that God has prepared for them.

Church Leaders: Although, this book deals with leadership in general. I must streamline on the leadership of the local church. From the associate pastors to lay leaders, their primary responsibility is to uphold the Senior Pastor's hand. They are to build with the head pastor as co-laborers.

The Senior Pastor follows Christ, receive instructions and directions from the Holy Spirit. And then pass it down to the leadership team who then implement this in the congregation.

In the next chapter we will move forward in this to discuss relationship building and limitations within the leadership of the local church that can easily bring disunity if not curbed.

CHAPTER THREE

BUILDING RELATIONSHIPS IN THE CHURCH

I believe so far we have done justice in the teaching of leadership principles for success in this book. Now, we must move forward to discuss in this chapter and the next, some key issues that must be noted if the leadership, especially within the local church will stand the test of time.

Although, team leadership helps to achieve the vision of the church, but we must understand within the leadership structure there must be some kind of restrictions and confinement as to how far people are allowed to implement or exercise their authority. Too many people step out of bound as a result of not understanding this principle. Some take advantage over those as a result of pride or ignorance.

Senior Pastor & Associates: The Senior Pastor or visionary who received the call to pioneer the church has the responsibility of casting the vision to the other Pastors, Ministers, Lay leaders, and members.

When the vision is eventually born, the Senior Pastor must take time to invest in his leadership team, especially the pastors and ministers serving with him. They determine how far the vision will grow.

The Senior Pastor must carry the other ministers along in his plans and vision. Because, most times when people are not carried along they tend to be reluctant in their passion for the ministry. The Senior Pastor has to be apostolic in his operation by releasing ministers to their ministries within the local church, and giving the necessary platform for them to carry out their ministries.

Most times, immature or upcoming ministers might take advantage over the Senior Pastor's generosity, especially if the younger minister has a visible spiritual gift. Senior Pastors must know when to draw the line, and set boundaries that shouldn't be crossed. Senior Pastors must know when it is time to release other ministers from under their leadership to higher level of commitment.

One philosophy I have adhered to, taught by a Spiritual father I cherish is that ministry is a Bus. And not everyone is destined to go with you to the end. You as the visionary must know when they get to their bus stop. Taking ministers or leaders past their bus stop will hinder the vision. They will be occupying the seat of another. Also they will be static and unproductive because their assignment is over. You must learn to release people at the appropriate time, and with the right heart.

Note that some leaders will always take advantage over you as the Senior Pastor. One thing is certain, you have a vision and that cannot be taken away.

Pastors and Lay Leaders: The same principle of investing in your leaders applies to this category as well. Too many leaders feel used by pastors. I once talked to a church leader who told me she will never serve in a small congregation again. I asked why? And she said she felt used by her Pastor. She said, most small churches want to use people to achieve their goals. But she will rather attend a mega church where they have sufficient people so she will not exhaust her life in a church and be eventually dropped or not appreciated. Wow!

That sounds familiar with many leaders. Pastors must take time to appreciate their leaders in any way they are capable. Appreciation goes a long way. It doesn't matter how much money it cost. If they are worth it, then, do it. Your leaders are your pillars. Remember, leaders most times are closer to the pews than the pastor. When Satan tries to attack a church, if he gets the leaders, then he can get the church. If your leadership team is intact, and members leave, give it some time it will bounce back up. Leaders can reproduce themselves if mentored right.

Pastoral Care: After much research, I discovered that it's the same song that is being sung everywhere you turn concerning pastors in dealing with members or leaders. One thing that is common is that pastors don't care enough for their members. A lady once told me that her pastor doesn't even know her name or anything about her. She had been one of the financial pillars of the church for some time. Later she decided to leave because it seemed to her pastor wanted was only interested in her money, and doesn't really care much about the affairs of her family.

I understand when a church is large in number; it could be hard for pastors to know everyone. That is why the Pastor must learn that leadership is delegation. If the Pastor does not have leaders, he should raise people into leadership position; otherwise he will either wear himself out or shipwreck his ministry eventually.

It is absurd for a Pastor to have a private jet, live in a multi-million dollar house, yet there are members of the church who cannot afford 3 square meals a day. That is wrong. I want pastors to prosper in every area of their lives. I believe ministers of the gospel deserve it because of the nature of the assignment. But, there must be a balance. The reason why tithing is such a huge problem for many today in America is as a result of the abuse some pastors have shown to their congregation.

The Pastor must show care in three major areas:
1. The spiritual life of the flock
2. Helping members fulfill their purpose for existence
3. Care for their physical needs when in desperate need (If the church has the money or resources needed).

Any church that does this will never die. Your members are your defense. Your leaders are your pillars.

Every year in our local churches that have the resources, we make sure that each member gets some kind of material gift or food for Christmas. Besides the season we give other gifts donated to the ministry during the course of the year. We try to maintain a storage unit to keep things, and give it out when there is a need. We do both in-reach and outreach. Some ministries concentrate only on the outreach part of the ministry and forget that there are people in the church as well that need help. There must be a balance in the ministry if you will be fruitful. Your church doesn't have to be big to do these things. You start with what you have and God will increase it.

In my apostolic assignment, I have helped pastors raised money in churches where they told me their members wouldn't support their ministry. I did this by the help of the Holy Spirit, and by simply applying the principles I have taught so far in this book.

One time I was invited to a church where the pastor was thinking of quitting the ministry. He was so frustrated financially. He was well situated in one of the wealthiest part of the country, yet his ministry suffered. After much prayer God revealed to me that his members have the resources to take the ministry to the next level, but the pastor lack the know-how of how vision connects to provision.

The people were used to pastors taking money from congregation without offering reasonable service, or fulfilling the ministry as promised. I got to the church and ministered about purpose and vision of a local church. Eventually the members saw they have hindered their church from fulfilling her purpose by not supporting the vision, hitherto hindering the overall vision of Jesus of reaching the world. And the pastor saw that he had held the people back by not casting the vision right. So they didn't see the reason why they should give their financial support.

There are two kinds of people every pastor will deal with: Those whom words can convince, and those whom only action will convince. Show people you care, and they will go all the way with you and for you.

We'll close this chapter by looking at what Jesus' ministry again:

> After these things Jesus went over the Sea of Galilee, which is the Sea of Tiberias. Then a great multitude followed Him, because they saw His signs which He performed on those who were diseased. And Jesus went up on the mountain, and there He sat with His disciples.
>
> Now the Passover, a feast of the Jews, was near. Then Jesus lifted up His eyes, and seeing a great multitude coming toward Him, He said to Philip, "Where shall we buy bread, that these may eat?" But this He said to test him, for He Himself knew what He would do.
>
> Philip answered Him, "Two hundred denarii worth of bread is not sufficient for them, that every one of them may have a little." One of His disciples, Andrew, Simon Peter's brother, said to Him, "There is a lad here who has five barley loaves and two small fish, but what are they among so many?"

Then Jesus said, "Make the people sit down." Now there was much grass in the place. So the men sat down, in number about five thousand. And Jesus took the loaves, and when He had given thanks He distributed them to the disciples, and the disciples to those sitting down; and likewise of the fish, as much as they wanted. So when they were filled, He said to His disciples, "Gather up the fragments that remain, so that nothing is lost." Therefore they gathered them up, and filled twelve baskets with the fragments of the five barley loaves which were left over by those who had eaten. Then those men, when they had seen the sign that Jesus did, said, "This is truly the Prophet who is to come into the world." John 6:1-14 NKJV.

CHAPTER FOUR

PRESERVING THE VISION

Leading people is not an easy task. It takes the grace of God. That is why one must be called into it. The devil will do everything possible to destroy the focus of the team. Most times the little things that we might take for granted are the very things the devil uses as a weapon of destruction. That is why prayer is so important for the leader. You cannot afford not to be prayerful. In my other book "Prayer that Touches Heaven", I taught about different kinds of Prayer.

Prayer Preserves:
One thing that is certain is that, Satan cannot destroy the vision of God. Because it is of God, but he does attack those who pursue the vision or carries out God's agenda. He does it in a very subtle way. *"And the Lord said, "Simon, Simon! Indeed, Satan has asked for you, that he may sift you as wheat.* ***But I have prayed for you****, that your faith should not fail; and when you have returned to Me, strengthen your brethren."* Luke 22:31,32 NKJV.

It is the leader's duty to pray for their team, so they are not outran by the enemy. One person in the group can make or mar the overall mission. And I think we should learn immensely from Joshua's leadership:

> But the Israelites were unfaithful in regard to the devoted things; Achan son of Karmi, the son of Zimri, the son of Zerah, of the tribe of Judah, took some of them. So the LORD's anger burned against Israel. Now Joshua sent men from Jericho to Ai, which is near Beth Aven to the east of Bethel, and told them, "Go up and spy out the region." So the men went up and spied out Ai. When they returned to Joshua, they said, "Not all the army will have to go up against Ai. Send two or three thousand men to take it and do not weary the whole army, for only a few people live there." So about three thousand went up; but they were routed by the men of Ai, who killed about thirty-six of them. They chased the Israelites from the city gate as far as the stone quarries and struck them down on the slopes. At this the hearts of the people melted in fear and became like water. Then Joshua tore his clothes and fell facedown to the ground before the ark of the

LORD, remaining there till evening. The elders of Israel did the same and sprinkled dust on their heads. And Joshua said, "Alas, Sovereign LORD, why did you ever bring this people across the Jordan to deliver us into the hands of the Amorites to destroy us? If only we had been content to stay on the other side of the Jordan! Pardon your servant, Lord. What can I say, now that Israel has been routed by its enemies? The Canaanites and the other people of the country will hear about this and they will surround us and wipe out our name from the earth. What then will you do for your own great name?"

The LORD said to Joshua, "Stand up! What are you doing down on your face? Israel has sinned; they have violated my covenant, which I commanded them to keep. They have taken some of the devoted things; they have stolen, they have lied, they have put them with their own possessions. That is why the Israelites cannot stand against their enemies; they turn their backs and run because they have been made liable to destruction. I will not be with you anymore unless you destroy whatever among you is devoted to destruction. "Go, consecrate the people. Tell them, 'Consecrate yourselves in preparation for tomorrow; for this is what the LORD, the God of Israel, says: There are devoted things among you, Israel. You cannot stand against your enemies until you remove them. "'In the morning, present yourselves tribe by tribe. The tribe the LORD chooses shall come forward clan by clan; the clan the LORD chooses shall come forward family by family; and the family the LORD chooses shall come forward man by man. Whoever is caught with the devoted things shall be destroyed by fire, along with all that belongs to him. He has violated the covenant of the LORD and has done an outrageous thing in Israel!'"

Early the next morning Joshua had Israel come forward by tribes, and Judah was chosen. The clans of Judah came forward, and the Zerahites were chosen. He had the clan of the Zerahites come forward by families, and Zimri was chosen. Joshua had his family come forward man by man, and Achan son of Karmi, the son of Zimri, the son of Zerah, of the tribe of Judah, was chosen. Then Joshua said to Achan, "My son, give glory to the LORD, the God of Israel, and honor him. Tell me what you have done; do not hide it from me."

Achan replied, "It is true! I have sinned against the LORD, the God of Israel. This is what I have done: When I saw in the plunder a beautiful robe from Babylonia, two hundred shekels of silver and a bar of gold weighing fifty shekels, I coveted them and took them. They are hidden in the ground inside my tent, with the silver underneath." So Joshua sent messengers, and they ran to the tent, and there it was, hidden in his tent, with the silver underneath. They took the things from the tent, brought them to Joshua and all the Israelites and spread them out before the LORD. Joshua 7:1-23.

One man, Achan, brought defeat to the whole people. Joshua didn't expect such defeat, he only sent a few people for this war against the nation of AI. He underestimated them for their size. Truthfully speaking, AI wasn't a big of a deal when it comes to war with the Israelites. If God could give them victory over Jericho, then AI is nothing. That would have been Joshua's thinking, except for the fact that, there was an open door in his leadership that hindered the victory.

This is one reason to be very prayerful when installing leaders in the ministry like Jesus did.

"One of those days Jesus went out to a mountainside to pray, and spent the night praying to God. When morning came, he called his disciples to him and chose twelve of them, whom he also designated apostles." Luke 6:12-13

One wrong person can cause life time havoc. I have seen leaders in a church who didn't like their pastor or pastor's decision. And thereafter refuse to support the church financially. Some leaders go to the extent of conniving with the members against the Pastor. Such pastor needs to call on the God of the vision for deliverance; otherwise, it will be only a matter of time, before the church will be gone. I have witnessed churches closed down because the leaders revolted against their pastors.

One thing visionary pastors needs to understand and underscore at the back of their mind is that the vision has a source. The day you think that you have gotten it together, under control, that day you predict your downfall. God's strength is revealed in our weaknesses, not our strength (2 Cor.12:9).

Most times it is impossible to know the heart of people before placing them in leadership, except what is revealed to you. Sincerely, not everything you will see or know spiritually as a pastor, because there are some lessons God wants to teach you at an appropriate time. So, don't beat yourself up that you made a mistake, if you are going through a rough time with your leadership. Remember Joshua went through it as seen earlier, Jesus went through this as well, betrayed by his very own disciple, Judas Iscariot (Luke 22:47,48).

Until you experience the kiss of Judas, you are not ready for the throne. Too many people quit because of disappointment they have experienced in their lives. But the truth is that, disappointment is part of the package for success and greatness. See my other book: "Destined for Greatness" for more enlightenment in this subject.

Little Foxes:

"Catch for us the foxes, the little foxes that ruin the vineyards, our vineyards that are in bloom."
Song of Solomon 2:15

We see King Solomon here in this paradoxical chapter, expressing love between the man and the woman, which a 'type' of God and his creation.

In the midst of the vine were thorns, foxes that destroyed the plant. Research shows that foxes like other animals causes damage in the agriculture sector all around the world, *"Foxes cause an estimated £12 million of damage."*[15]

Now, that estimated figure converted in dollars will be 18 plus million dollars, of damage caused by a fox. Yet, the fox has its own purpose in creation.

Every religious organization attracts foxes. You cannot rule them out, but you can curb them, control them, and weed them out from time to time. This can also be likened to Satanic influences in the Church or ministry. If you ignore them you will end up in disarray. Some of key signs are:

1. **Jealousy & Envy Amongst Leaders**: There is nothing as dangerous as this. Jealousy will lead to envy. Envy to bitterness. When it gets to the level of bitterness, it has become a stronghold in the life of the individual. Anything demonic, disastrous is expected at this level. Every Leader should do whatever they can to uproot the seed of jealousy from their midst.

2. **Gossip**: This is another epidemic within the church today. Gossip within leadership can spread like a wild fire into the congregation which can turn the hearts of the people especially young believer's heart in the wrong direction.

   Gossip circulates when the truth is not known; people will generally assume the wrong thing.

   One time Satan tried using this tool to destroy the church I pastored, and I try informing my leaders with the necessary information, but this virus had already spread to the members. The only way I could cure it was to come before the members and declared the truth. You never know who is saying what. You have to be ready to tell your members exactly what is going on. Don't keep them assuming.

3. **Secret Meetings:** This is another area to watch out for, especially if the ministry operates in the prophetic. Every prophetic ministry attracts the spirit of Jezebel and Jehu. Every apostolic ministry attracts the spirit of Absalom.

   Their mission is to overrule and overturn God's agenda. These people will call for meetings not authorized by the Pastor, Elders trying to control the church, etc. This is nothing but the Devil doing his destructive ministry through those who have opened themselves up to him.

These are key areas Pastors and Visionaries need to watch out. There are ways to deal with these issues. You must remember they have spiritual origin, so deal with it spiritually first before the physical.

Confronting Issues Spiritually:

Do it in prayer. This is how you pray:

1. Call on the God who gave the vision. Let Him know you have committed the vision, church, ministry in His hands for sustenance. Therefore every other god must be disposed.
2. Uproot in prayer every demonic forces assigned to the vision. Bind them in the Name of Jesus, declare their assignments aborted in Jesus Name
3. Pray that God disconnect the wrong people from your lives and group.
4. Uproot the evil seed sown into the hearts of the right people God ordained for you. Uproot also the evil seed sown into the ministry, church, and

organization. Uproot them and burn them with fire spiritually.

5. Declare in the Name of Jesus that every door that has been opened from the kingdom of darkness be shut by the power of Holy Spirit in Jesus Name.
6. Release the blood of Jesus over your group and release the power in the blood of Jesus to bring restoration, healing and deliverance to your organization.
7. Build a wall of fire and protection around you and ministry in the Name of Jesus. Disperse ministering angels assigned to the vision to keep watch on the ministry.

Confronting Issues Physically:

After you've done your homework spiritually there are things the Holy Spirit might lead you to do. Some of which will be confronting the people involved.

I have met with some leaders, pastors who have been too soft and have likened that to gentleness as a spiritual fruit. That is not true, especially when the Kingdom of God is in jeopardy. It is intimidation of the Devil against your emotions. You have to learn to confront issues with the guidance of the Holy Spirit. *"For God has not given us a spirit of fear, but of power and of love and of a sound mind."* 2 Timothy 1:7

Jesus, while on earth had to confront people and issues. He dealt with them and didn't let things that could jeopardize the Kingdom slide through:

"Then Jesus went into the temple of God and drove out all those who bought and sold in the temple, and overturned the tables of the money changers and the seats of those who sold doves. And He said to them, "It is written, 'My house shall be called a house of prayer,' but you have made it a 'den of thieves.' Matthew 21:12-13

> *"So when they continued asking Him, He raised Himself up and said to them, "He who is without sin among you, let him throw a stone at her first." And again He stooped down and wrote on the ground. Then those who heard it, being convicted by their conscience, went out one by one, beginning with the oldest even to the last. And Jesus was left alone, and the woman standing in the midst".*
> John 8:7-9

I must stress here that there has to be balance to this. There are people that you need to confront when led, and there are those that you allow the Holy Spirit to handle Himself, like that of Moses:

> *Now it came to pass, as he finished speaking all these words, that the ground split apart under them, and the earth opened its mouth and swallowed them up, with their households and all the men with Korah, with all their goods. So they and all those with them went down alive into the pit; the earth closed over them, and they perished from among the assembly. Then all Israel who were around them fled at their cry, for they said, "Lest the earth swallow us up also!"*
>
> *And a fire came out from the LORD and consumed the two hundred and fifty men who were offering incense.* Numbers 16:31-35

You must let the Lord lead you at all times in your service. Eventually, you will see His manifestation on your behalf. I believe I have done justice in this teaching of transformational leadership. Apply what you have learnt so far, and I guarantee you will succeed in your leadership venture.

Father I pray for all that have read and meditated on these words, message you placed in my heart for your servants. Lord, let their lives never remain the same again. Cause your revival fire fall upon them and their leadership. Let all barriers to success be taken out. And release uncommon grace for uncommon achievements upon them for your name sake in Jesus Name.
Amen.

Other Books By Dr. George Agbonson:

Journey of Faith

Prayer that Touches Heaven

Destined For Greatness

Contact:

Christ Restoration Ministries Int'L.
U.S.A
www.christrestoration.net
Email: admin@christrestoration.net

BIBLOGRAPHY

1. Blackaby, Henry T.; Richard Blackaby. *Spiritual Leadership: Moving People on to God's Agenda.* Broadman & Holman Publishers. Kindle Edition. 2001
2. Wilkes, C. Gene. *Jesus On Leadership.* Carol Stream, Tyndale House Publishers, Inc. 1998
3. Keener, S. Craig. *The Bible Background Commentary New Testament.* Downers Grove, InterVarsity Press. 1993
4. Sanders, Oswald. *Spiritual Leadership.* Chicago, Moody Publishers. 2007
5. Ibid. Pg. 28
6. Morris, K. Gregory. *In Pursuit Of Leadershp.* Maitland, Xulon Press. 2006
7. Ibid, Keener, S. Craig. Pg.626
8. Cope, Landa. *An Introduction to The Old Testament Template.* Burtigny, The Template Institute Press. 2006
9. Kendall, R.T. *The Anointing: Yesterday, Today, Tomorrow.* Lake Mary, Charisma House. 2003
10. Ibid, Pg. 14

11. Hinn, Benny. *Angels And Demons.* Charlotte, Life Bridge Books. 2011
12. Ibid, Pg. 38
13. Ibid, Pg. 22
14. Keller W. Phillip. *A Shepherd Looks at Psalm 23.* Grand Rapids, Zondervan. 1970
15. www.thefoxwebsite.org Foxes and Agriculture: Overview. Copyright 2007-2008 The Fox Website. Site maintained by the Mammal Group, University of Bristol.

www.ingramcontent.com/pod-product-compliance
Lightning Source LLC
Chambersburg PA
CBHW071123090426
42736CB00012B/1996